I0275530

MznLnx

Missing Links Exam Preps

Exam Prep for

Management: Meeting and Exceeding Customer Expectations

Plunkett, Attner, & Allen, 9th Edition

The MznLnx Exam Prep is your link from the texbook and lecture to your exams.
The MznLnx Exam Preps are unauthorized and comprehensive reviews of your textbooks.

All material provided by MznLnx and Rico Publications (c) 2010
Textbook publishers and textbook authors do not particpate in or contribute to these reviews.

MznLnx

Rico
Publications

Exam Prep for Management: Meeting and Exceeding Customer Expectations
9th Edition
Plunkett, Attner, & Allen

Publisher: Raymond Houge
Assistant Editor: Michael Rouger
Text and Cover Designer: Lisa Buckner
Marketing Manager: Sara Swagger
Project Manager, Editorial Production: Jerry Emerson
Art Director: Vernon Lowerui
Product Manager: Dave Mason
Editorial Assitant: Rachel Guzmanji
Pedagogy: Debra Long
Cover Image: Jim Reed/Getty Images
Text and Cover Printer: City Printing, Inc.
Compositor: Media Mix, Inc.

(c) 2010 Rico Publications
ALL RIGHTS RESERVED. No part of this work covered by the copyright may be reproduced or used in any form or by an means--graphic, electronic, or mechanical, including photocopying, recording, taping, Web distribution, information storage, and retrieval systems, or in any other manner--without the written permission of the publisher.

For more information about our products, contact us at:
Dave.Mason@RicoPublications.com

For permission to use material from this text or product, submit a request online to:
Dave.Mason@RicoPublications.com

Printed in the United States
ISBN:

Contents

TO THE STUDENT

COMPREHENSIVE

The *MznLnx* Exam Prep series is designed to help you pass your exams. Editors at MznLnx review your textbooks and then prepare these practice exams to help you master the textbook material. Unlike study guides, workbooks, and practice tests provided by the texbook publisher and textbook authors, *MznLnx* gives you ***all*** of the material in each chapter in exam form, not just samples, so you can be sure to nail your exam.

MECHANICAL

The MznLnx Exam Prep series creates exams that will help you learn the subject matter as well as test you on your understanding. Each question is designed to help you master the concept. Just working through the exams, you gain an understanding of the subject--its a simple mechanical process that produces success.

INTEGRATED STUDY GUIDE AND REVIEW

MznLnx is not just a set of exams designed to test you, its also a comprehensive review of the subject content. Each exam question is also a review of the concept, making sure that you will get the answer correct without having to go to other sources of material. You learn as you go! Its the easiest way to pass an exam.

HUMOR

Studying can be tedious and dry. MznLnx's instructional design includes moderate humor within the exam questions on occassion, to break the tedium and revitalize the brain

1. _________ was a writer, management consultant, and self-described 'social ecologist.' Widely considered to be 'the father of modern management,' his 39 books and countless scholarly and popular articles explored how humans are organized across all sectors of society--in business, government and the nonprofit world. His writings have predicted many of the major developments of the late twentieth century, including privatization and decentralization; the rise of Japan to economic world power; the decisive importance of marketing; and the emergence of the information society with its necessity of lifelong learning. In 1959, Drucker coined the term 'knowledge worker' and later in his life considered knowledge work productivity to be the next frontier of management.

a. Peter Ferdinand Drucker
b. Chrissie Hynde
c. Jacques Al-Salawat Nasruddin Nasser
d. Debora L. Spar

2. _________, a business term, is a measure of how products and services supplied by a company meet or surpass customer expectation. It is seen as a key performance indicator within business and is part of the four perspectives of a Balanced Scorecard.

In a competitive marketplace where businesses compete for customers, _________ is seen as a key differentiator and increasingly has become a key element of business strategy.

a. Foreign ownership
b. Horizontal integration
c. Customer satisfaction
d. Critical Success Factor

3. _________ is a technical term used in management science popularized by Joseph M. Juran

He defined an internal and external customers as anyone affected by the product or by the process used to produce the product, in the context of quality management. _________s may play the role as supplier, processer, and customer in the sequence of product development.

He claimed that the organization must understand and identify both internal and external customers and their needs.

a. Internal customer
b. AAAI
c. A Stake in the Outcome
d. A4e

4. _________ consists of the processes a company uses to track and organize its contacts with its current and prospective customers. _________ software is used to support these processes; information about customers and customer interactions can be entered, stored and accessed by employees in different company departments. Typical _________ goals are to improve services provided to customers, and to use customer contact information for targeted marketing.

a. Green marketing
b. Disruptive technology
c. Marketing plan
d. Customer relationship management

5. _________, commonly known as e-commerce, consists of the buying and selling of products or services over electronic systems such as the Internet and other computer networks. The amount of trade conducted electronically has grown extraordinarily with widespread Internet usage. The use of commerce is conducted in this way, spurring and drawing on innovations in electronic funds transfer, supply chain management, Internet marketing, online transaction processing, electronic data interchange (EDI), inventory management systems, and automated data collection systems.

a. Electronic commerce
b. Online shopping
c. A4e
d. A Stake in the Outcome

6. _________ is the temporary suspension or permanent termination of employment of an employee or (more commonly) a group of employees for business reasons, such as the decision that certain positions are no longer necessary or a business slow-down or interruption in work. Originally the term '_________' referred exclusively to a temporary interruption in work, as when factory work cyclically falls off. However, in recent times the term can also refer to the permanent elimination of a position.

a. Wrongful dismissal
b. Termination of employment
c. Retirement
d. Layoff

7. _________ has been described as the 'process of social influence in which one person can enlist the aid and support of others in the accomplishment of a common task' . A definition more inclusive of followers comes from Alan Keith of Genentech who said '_________ is ultimately about creating a way for people to contribute to making something extraordinary happen.'

_________ is one of the most salient aspects of the organizational context. However, defining _________ has been challenging.

a. 1990 Clean Air Act
b. Situational leadership
c. 28-hour day
d. Leadership

8. _________ is a method of direct marketing in which a salesperson solicits to prospective customers to buy products or services, either over the phone or through a subsequent face to face or Web conferencing appointment scheduled during the call.

_________ can also include recorded sales pitches programmed to be played over the phone via automatic dialing. _________ has come under fire in recent years, being viewed as an annoyance by many.

a. 28-hour day
b. 33 Strategies of War
c. 1990 Clean Air Act
d. Telemarketing

9. The general definition of an _________ is an evaluation of a person, organization, system, process, project or product. _________s are performed to ascertain the validity and reliability of information; also to provide an assessment of a system's internal control. The goal of an _________ is to express an opinion on the person / organization/system (etc) in question, under evaluation based on work done on a test basis.

a. Internal control
b. A Stake in the Outcome
c. Audit
d. Audit committee

10. The 'business case for _________', theorizes that in a global marketplace, a company that employs a diverse workforce (both men and women, people of many generations, people from ethnically and racially diverse backgrounds etc.) is better able to understand the demographics of the marketplace it serves and is thus better equipped to thrive in that marketplace than a company that has a more limited range of employee demographics.

An additional corollary suggests that a company that supports the _________ of its workforce can also improve employee satisfaction, productivity and retention.

a. Trademark
b. Virtual team
c. Diversity
d. Kanban

11. _________ is exchange of capital, goods, and services across international borders or territories. In most countries, it represents a significant share of gross domestic product (GDP.) While _________ has been present throughout much of history , its economic, social, and political importance has been on the rise in recent centuries.

a. International Trade
b. AAAI
c. A Stake in the Outcome
d. A4e

12. _________ or lean production, which is often known simply as 'Lean', is a production practice that considers the expenditure of resources for any goal other than the creation of value for the end customer to be wasteful, and thus a target for elimination. Working from the perspective of the customer who consumes a product or service, 'value' is defined as any action or process that a customer would be willing to pay for. Basically, lean is centered around creating more value with less work.

a. Six Sigma
b. Production line
c. Theory of constraints
d. Lean Manufacturing

13. _________ can be regarded as an outcome of mental processes (cognitive process) leading to the selection of a course of action among several alternatives. Every _________ process produces a final choice. The output can be an action or an opinion of choice.

a. 1990 Clean Air Act
b. 28-hour day
c. Decision making
d. 33 Strategies of War

14. _________ for short is a descriptive term for certain executives in a business operation. It is also a formal title held by some business executives, most commonly in the hospitality industry.

A _________ has broad, overall responsibility for a business or organization. Whereas a manager may be responsible for one functional area, the _________ is responsible for all areas.

a. Chief knowledge officer
b. Chief technology officer
c. General manager
d. Managing director

15. A _________ is a list of the general tasks and responsibilities of a position. Typically, it also includes to whom the position reports, specifications such as the qualifications needed by the person in the job, salary range for the position, etc. A _________ is usually developed by conducting a job analysis, which includes examining the tasks and sequences of tasks necessary to perform the job.

a. Recruitment
b. Recruitment Process Insourcing
c. Job description
d. Recruitment advertising

16. _________ is the strategic and coherent approach to the management of an organisation's most valued assets - the people working there who individually and collectively contribute to the achievement of the objectives of the business. The terms '_________' and 'human resources' (HR) have largely replaced the term 'personnel management' as a description of the processes involved in managing people in organizations. In simple sense, _________ means employing people, developing their resources, utilizing, maintaining and compensating their services in tune with the job and organizational requirement.

a. Human resource management
b. Revolving door syndrome
c. Progressive discipline
d. Job knowledge

17. _________ is an integrated communications-based process through which individuals and communities discover that existing and newly-identified needs and wants may be satisfied by the products and services of others.

_________ is defined by the American _________ Association as the activity, set of institutions, and processes for creating, communicating, delivering, and exchanging offerings that have value for customers, clients, partners, and society at large. The term developed from the original meaning which referred literally to going to market, as in shopping, or going to a market to buy or sell goods or services.

a. Market development
b. Disruptive technology
c. Customer relationship management
d. Marketing

18. _________ is one of the managerial functions like planning, organizing, staffing and directing. It is an important function because it helps to check the errors and to take the corrective action so that deviation from standards are minimized and stated goals of the organization are achieved in desired manner.According to modern concepts, _________ is a foreseeing action whereas earlier concept of _________ was used only when errors were detected. _________ in management means setting standards, measuring actual performance and taking corrective action.

a. Schedule of reinforcement
b. Turnover
c. Decision tree pruning
d. Control

19. _________ is a contract between two parties, one being the employer and the other being the employee. An employee may be defined as: 'A person in the service of another under any contract of hire, express or implied, oral or written, where the employer has the power or right to control and direct the employee in the material details of how the work is to be performed.' Black's Law Dictionary page 471 (5th ed. 1979.)

a. Employment counsellor
b. Exit interview
c. Employment
d. Employment rate

20. In politics, a _________, (by metaphor with the carved _________ at the prow of a sailing ship), is a person who holds an important title or office yet executes little actual power, most commonly limited by convention rather than law. Common _________s include constitutional monarchs, such as: Queen Elizabeth II, the Emperor of Japan, or presidents in parliamentary democracies, such as the President of Israel.

While the authority of a _________ is in practice generally symbolic, public opinion, respect for the office or the office holder and access to high levels of government can give them significant influence on events.

a. 28-hour day
b. Figurehead
c. 1990 Clean Air Act
d. 33 Strategies of War

21. The _________ was a period in the late 18th and early 19th centuries when major changes in agriculture, manufacturing, mining, and transportation had a profound effect on the socioeconomic and cultural conditions in Britain. The changes subsequently spread throughout Europe, North America, and eventually the world. The onset of the _________ marked a major turning point in human society; almost every aspect of daily life was eventually influenced in some way.

a. Affiliation
b. Abraham Harold Maslow
c. Industrial Revolution
d. Adam Smith

22. _________ is a business management strategy, initially implemented by Motorola, that today enjoys widespread application in many sectors of industry.

_________ seeks to improve the quality of process outputs by identifying and removing the causes of defects (errors) and variation in manufacturing and business processes. It uses a set of quality management methods, including statistical methods, and creates a special infrastructure of people within the organization ('Black Belts' etc.)

a. Production line
b. Takt time
c. Theory of constraints
d. Six Sigma

23. In economics, _________ is the desire to own something and the ability to pay for it. The term _________ signifies the ability or the willingness to buy a particular commodity at a given point of time.

a. 33 Strategies of War
b. 28-hour day
c. 1990 Clean Air Act
d. Demand

24. An _________ is a person who has possession of an enterprise and assumes significant accountability for the inherent risks and the outcome. It is an ambitious leader who combines land, labor, and capital to create and market new goods or services. The term is a loanword from French and was first defined by the Irish economist Richard Cantillon.

a. A Stake in the Outcome
b. A4e
c. AAAI
d. Entrepreneur

25. _________ refers to an individual's desire for significant accomplishment, mastering of skills, control, or high standards. The term was introduced by the psychologist, David McClelland.

_________ is related to the difficulty of tasks people choose to undertake.

a. Need for power
b. Need for achievement
c. 1990 Clean Air Act
d. Two-factor theory

1. The 'business case for _________', theorizes that in a global marketplace, a company that employs a diverse workforce (both men and women, people of many generations, people from ethnically and racially diverse backgrounds etc.) is better able to understand the demographics of the marketplace it serves and is thus better equipped to thrive in that marketplace than a company that has a more limited range of employee demographics.

An additional corollary suggests that a company that supports the _________ of its workforce can also improve employee satisfaction, productivity and retention.

a. Trademark
b. Virtual team
c. Diversity
d. Kanban

2. The _________ was a period in the late 18th and early 19th centuries when major changes in agriculture, manufacturing, mining, and transportation had a profound effect on the socioeconomic and cultural conditions in Britain. The changes subsequently spread throughout Europe, North America, and eventually the world. The onset of the _________ marked a major turning point in human society; almost every aspect of daily life was eventually influenced in some way.

a. Industrial Revolution
b. Adam Smith
c. Abraham Harold Maslow
d. Affiliation

3. _________ or lean production, which is often known simply as 'Lean', is a production practice that considers the expenditure of resources for any goal other than the creation of value for the end customer to be wasteful, and thus a target for elimination. Working from the perspective of the customer who consumes a product or service, 'value' is defined as any action or process that a customer would be willing to pay for. Basically, lean is centered around creating more value with less work.

a. Six Sigma
b. Production line
c. Theory of constraints
d. Lean Manufacturing

4. A _________ is the term given to a company that facilitates the learning of its members and continuously transforms itself. _________s develop as a result of the pressures facing modern organizations and enables them to remain competitive in the business environment. A _________ has five main features; systems thinking, personal mastery, mental models, shared vision and team learning.

a. Hoshin Kanri
b. Quality function deployment
c. 1990 Clean Air Act
d. Learning organization

5. _________, widely known as F. W. Taylor, was an American mechanical engineer who sought to improve industrial efficiency. He is regarded as the father of scientific management, and was one of the first management consultants.

Taylor was one of the intellectual leaders of the Efficiency Movement and his ideas, broadly conceived, were highly influential in the Progressive Era.

a. Geoffrey Colvin
b. Douglas N. Daft
c. Jonah Jacob Goldberg
d. Frederick Winslow Taylor

6. _________ is a contract between two parties, one being the employer and the other being the employee. An employee may be defined as: 'A person in the service of another under any contract of hire, express or implied, oral or written, where the employer has the power or right to control and direct the employee in the material details of how the work is to be performed.' Black's Law Dictionary page 471 (5th ed. 1979.)

a. Employment counsellor
b. Exit interview
c. Employment rate
d. Employment

7. The term _________ was created by President Lyndon B. Johnson when he signed Executive Order 11246 on September 24, 1965, created to prohibit federal contractors from discriminating against employees on the basis of race, sex, creed, religion, color, or national origin. In more recent times, most employers have also added sexual orientation to the list of non-discrimination.

The Executive Order also required contractors to implement affirmative action plans to increase the participation of minorities and women in the workplace.

a. Equal employment opportunity
b. AAAI
c. A Stake in the Outcome
d. A4e

8. A _________ is a list of the general tasks and responsibilities of a position. Typically, it also includes to whom the position reports, specifications such as the qualifications needed by the person in the job, salary range for the position, etc. A _________ is usually developed by conducting a job analysis, which includes examining the tasks and sequences of tasks necessary to perform the job.

a. Recruitment
b. Recruitment Process Insourcing
c. Recruitment advertising
d. Job description

9. The _________ 1970 is an Act of the United Kingdom Parliament which prohibits any less favourable treatment between men and women in terms of pay and conditions of employment. It came into force on 29 December 1975. The term pay is interpreted in a broad sense to include, on top of wages, things like holidays, pension rights, company perks and some kinds of bonuses.

a. Australian labour law
b. Equal Pay Act
c. Oncale v. Sundowner Offshore Services
d. Architectural Barriers Act of 1968

10. _________ is the process by which the activities of an organisation, particularly those regarding decision-making, become concentrated within a particular location and/or group.

a. Product innovation
b. Chief operating officer
c. Centralization
d. Corner office

11. _________ is an organization's process of defining its strategy and making decisions on allocating its resources to pursue this strategy, including its capital and people. Various business analysis techniques can be used in _________, including SWOT analysis (Strengths, Weaknesses, Opportunities, and Threats) and PEST analysis (Political, Economic, Social, and Technological analysis) or STEER analysis involving Socio-cultural, Technological, Economic, Ecological, and Regulatory factors and EPISTEL (Environment, Political, Informatic, Social, Technological, Economic and Legal)

_________ is the formal consideration of an organization's future course. All _________ deals with at least one of three key questions:

1. 'What do we do?'
2. 'For whom do we do it?'
3. 'How do we excel?'

In business _________, the third question is better phrased 'How can we beat or avoid competition?'. (Bradford and Duncan, page 1.)

a. 28-hour day
b. 33 Strategies of War
c. Strategic planning
d. 1990 Clean Air Act

12. _________ or specialization is the specialization of cooperative labour in specific, circumscribed tasks and roles, intended to increase the productivity of labour. Historically the growth of a more and more complex _________ is closely associated with the growth of total output and trade, the rise of capitalism, and of the complexity of industrialization processes. Later, the _________ reached the level of a scientifically-based management practice with the time and motion studies associated with Taylorism.

a. Departmentalization
b. PATCOB
c. Division of labour
d. Labor force

13. The _________ is a standardized, on-scene, all-hazard incident management concept. It is a management protocol originally designed for emergency management agencies in the United States which was later federalized there. It has since been adopted by agencies in other countries.

a. Incident Command Structure
b. AAAI
c. A Stake in the Outcome
d. A4e

14. _________ and Theory Y are theories of human motivation created and developed by Douglas McGregor at the MIT Sloan School of Management in the 1960s that have been used in human resource management, organizational behavior, organizational communication and organizational development. They describe two very different attitudes toward workforce motivation. McGregor felt that companies followed either one or the other approach.

In _________, which many managers practice, management assumes employees are inherently lazy and will avoid work if they can. They inherently dislike work. Because of this, workers need to be closely supervised and comprehensive systems of controls developed.

a. Job enrichment
b. Cash cow
c. Theory X
d. Management team

15. Theory X and _________ are theories of human motivation created and developed by Douglas McGregor at the MIT Sloan School of Management in the 1960s that have been used in human resource management, organizational behavior, organizational communication and organizational development. They describe two very different attitudes toward workforce motivation. McGregor felt that companies followed either one or the other approach.

In _________, management assumes employees may be ambitious and self-motivated and exercise self-control. It is believed that employees enjoy their mental and physical work duties.

a. Contingency theory
b. Business Workflow Analysis
c. Design leadership
d. Theory Y

16. Maslow's _________ is a theory in psychology, proposed by Abraham Maslow in his 1943 paper A Theory of Human Motivation, which he subsequently extended to include his observations of humans' innate curiosity.

Maslow's _________ is predetermined in order of importance. It is often depicted as a pyramid consisting of five levels: the lowest level is associated with physiological needs, while the uppermost level is associated with self-actualization needs, particularly those related to identity and purpose. Deficiency needs must be met first. Once these are met, seeking to satisfy growth needs drives personal growth. The higher needs in this hierarchy only come into focus when the lower needs in the pyramid are met.

a. 33 Strategies of War
b. 1990 Clean Air Act
c. 28-hour day
d. Hierarchy of needs

17. _________ is a business management strategy aimed at embedding awareness of quality in all organizational processes. _________ has been widely used in manufacturing, education, hospitals, call centers, government, and service industries, as well as NASA space and science programs.

As defined by the International Organization for Standardization (ISO):

> '_________ is a management approach for an organization, centered on quality, based on the participation of all its members and aiming at long-term success through customer satisfaction, and benefits to all members of the organization and to society.' ISO 8402:1994

One major aim is to reduce variation from every process so that greater consistency of effort is obtained. (Royse, D., Thyer, B., Padgett D., ' Logan T., 2006)

a. 28-hour day
b. 1990 Clean Air Act
c. Total quality management
d. Quality management

18. _________, is the discipline of using scientific research-based principles, strategies, and other analytical methods, such as mathematical modeling to improve any organization's ability to enact rational, meaningful business management decisions.

a. Cross ownership
b. Management science
c. Trustee
d. Workflow

19. _________ in the USA, Canada, South Africa and Australia, and operational research in Europe, is an interdisciplinary branch of applied mathematics and formal science that uses methods such as mathematical modeling, statistics, and algorithms to arrive at optimal or near optimal solutions to complex problems. It is typically concerned with optimizing the maxima (profit, assembly line performance, crop yield, bandwidth, etc) or minima (loss, risk, etc.) of some objective function.

a. AAAI
b. A Stake in the Outcome
c. Operations research
d. A4e

20. A _________ is a subset of the overall internal controls of a business covering the application of people, documents, technologies, and procedures by management accountants to solving business problems such as costing a product, service or a business-wide strategy. _________s are distinct from regular information systems in that they are used to analyze other information systems applied in operational activities in the organization. Academically, the term is commonly used to refer to the group of information management methods tied to the automation or support of human decision making, e.g. Decision Support Systems, Expert systems, and Executive information systems.

a. 28-hour day
b. Strategic information system
c. 1990 Clean Air Act
d. Management information system

21. _________ is an interdisciplinary field of science and the study of the nature of complex systems in nature, society, and science. More specifically, it is a framework by which one can analyze and/or describe any group of objects that work in concert to produce some result. This could be a single organism, any organization or society, or any electro-mechanical or informational artifact.

a. 1990 Clean Air Act
b. 28-hour day
c. Systems thinking
d. Systems theory

22. _________ is the term used to describe a situation where different entities cooperate advantageously for a final outcome. Simply defined, it means that the whole is greater than the sum of the individual parts. Although the whole will be greater than each individual part, this is not the concept of _________.

a. Synergy
b. 1990 Clean Air Act
c. 33 Strategies of War
d. 28-hour day

23. _________ is a Japanese philosophy that focuses on continuous improvement throughout all aspects of life. When applied to the workplace, _________ activities continually improve all functions of a business, from manufacturing to management and from the CEO to the assembly line workers. By improving standardized activities and processes, _________ aims to eliminate waste .

a. Kaizen
b. Psychological pricing
c. Sensitivity analysis
d. Cross-docking

24. _________ is a company-wide computer software system used to manage and coordinate all the resources, information, and functions of a business from shared data stores.

An _________ system has a service-oriented architecture with modular hardware and software units and 'services' that communicate on a local area network. The modular design allows a business to add or reconfigure modules (perhaps from different vendors) while preserving data integrity in one shared database that may be centralized or distributed.

a. A4e
b. AAAI
c. Enterprise resource planning
d. A Stake in the Outcome

25. _________ can be considered to have three main components: quality control, quality assurance and quality improvement. _________ is focused not only on product quality, but also the means to achieve it. _________ therefore uses quality assurance and control of processes as well as products to achieve more consistent quality.

a. 1990 Clean Air Act
b. Total quality management
c. Quality management
d. 28-hour day

26. The _________ Automobile Company is an automobile manufacturer based in Wolfsburg, Germany, and is the original brand within the _________ Group, as well as the largest brand by sales volume.

_________ means 'people's car' in German, in which it is pronounced . Its current tagline or slogan is Das Auto .

a. Turnover
b. Rate of return
c. Competence-based Strategic Management
d. Volkswagen

27. _________ is the temporary suspension or permanent termination of employment of an employee or (more commonly) a group of employees for business reasons, such as the decision that certain positions are no longer necessary or a business slow-down or interruption in work. Originally the term '_________' referred exclusively to a temporary interruption in work, as when factory work cyclically falls off. However, in recent times the term can also refer to the permanent elimination of a position.

a. Termination of employment
b. Layoff
c. Wrongful dismissal
d. Retirement

28. _________ consists of the processes a company uses to track and organize its contacts with its current and prospective customers. _________ software is used to support these processes; information about customers and customer interactions can be entered, stored and accessed by employees in different company departments. Typical _________ goals are to improve services provided to customers, and to use customer contact information for targeted marketing.

a. Green marketing
b. Marketing plan
c. Disruptive technology
d. Customer relationship management

29. _________ is exchange of capital, goods, and services across international borders or territories. In most countries, it represents a significant share of gross domestic product (GDP.) While _________ has been present throughout much of history , its economic, social, and political importance has been on the rise in recent centuries.

a. AAAI
b. A Stake in the Outcome
c. A4e
d. International Trade

30. _________ is one of the managerial functions like planning, organizing, staffing and directing. It is an important function because it helps to check the errors and to take the corrective action so that deviation from standards are minimized and stated goals of the organization are achieved in desired manner.According to modern concepts, _________ is a foreseeing action whereas earlier concept of _________ was used only when errors were detected. _________ in management means setting standards, measuring actual performance and taking corrective action.

a. Schedule of reinforcement
b. Decision tree pruning
c. Turnover
d. Control

31. _________ is an American writer on business management practices, best-known for, In Search of Excellence (co-authored with Robert H. Waterman, Jr.)

Peters was born in Baltimore, Maryland. He went to Severn School for High School and attended Cornell University, receiving a bachelor's degree in civil engineering in 1965, and a master's degree in 1966.

a. Abraham Harold Maslow
b. Adam Smith
c. Affiliation
d. Thomas J. Peters

32. _________ refers to the movement of cash into or out of a business or financial product. It is usually measured during a specified, finite period of time. Measurement of _________ can be used

- to determine a project's rate of return or value. The time of _________s into and out of projects are used as inputs in financial models such as internal rate of return, and net present value.
- to determine problems with a business's liquidity. Being profitable does not necessarily mean being liquid. A company can fail because of a shortage of cash, even while profitable.
- as an alternate measure of a business's profits when it is believed that accrual accounting concepts do not represent economic realities. For example, a company may be notionally profitable but generating little operational cash (as may be the case for a company that barters its products rather than selling for cash.) In such a case, the company may be deriving additional operating cash by issuing shares evaluating default risk, re-investment requirements, etc.

_________ is a generic term used differently depending on the context. It may be defined by users for their own purposes.

a. Gross profit margin
b. Sweat equity
c. Cash flow
d. Gross profit

1. _________ is a form of applied ethics that examines ethical principles and moral or ethical problems that arise in a business environment. It applies to all aspects of business conduct and is relevant to the conduct of individuals and business organizations as a whole. Applied ethics is a field of ethics that deals with ethical questions in many fields such as medical, technical, legal and _________.

a. Corporate Sustainability
b. Facilitation payments
c. Hypernorms
d. Business ethics

2. The _________ was a period in the late 18th and early 19th centuries when major changes in agriculture, manufacturing, mining, and transportation had a profound effect on the socioeconomic and cultural conditions in Britain. The changes subsequently spread throughout Europe, North America, and eventually the world. The onset of the _________ marked a major turning point in human society; almost every aspect of daily life was eventually influenced in some way.

a. Abraham Harold Maslow
b. Adam Smith
c. Industrial Revolution
d. Affiliation

3. _________, commonly known as e-commerce, consists of the buying and selling of products or services over electronic systems such as the Internet and other computer networks. The amount of trade conducted electronically has grown extraordinarily with widespread Internet usage. The use of commerce is conducted in this way, spurring and drawing on innovations in electronic funds transfer, supply chain management, Internet marketing, online transaction processing, electronic data interchange (EDI), inventory management systems, and automated data collection systems.

a. A4e
b. Online shopping
c. Electronic commerce
d. A Stake in the Outcome

4. _________ or lean production, which is often known simply as 'Lean', is a production practice that considers the expenditure of resources for any goal other than the creation of value for the end customer to be wasteful, and thus a target for elimination. Working from the perspective of the customer who consumes a product or service, 'value' is defined as any action or process that a customer would be willing to pay for. Basically, lean is centered around creating more value with less work.

a. Lean Manufacturing
b. Six Sigma
c. Theory of constraints
d. Production line

5. _________ is the temporary suspension or permanent termination of employment of an employee or (more commonly) a group of employees for business reasons, such as the decision that certain positions are no longer necessary or a business slow-down or interruption in work. Originally the term '_________' referred exclusively to a temporary interruption in work, as when factory work cyclically falls off. However, in recent times the term can also refer to the permanent elimination of a position.

a. Termination of employment
b. Layoff
c. Retirement
d. Wrongful dismissal

6. _________ is a layer of management in an organization whose primary job responsibility is to monitor activities of subordinates while reporting to upper management.

In pre-computer times, _________ would collect information from junior management and reassemble it for senior management. With the advent of inexpensive PCs this function has been taken over by e-business systems.

a. Middle management
b. Theory Y
c. Continuous monitoring
d. Community management

7. _________ is one of the managerial functions like planning, organizing, staffing and directing. It is an important function because it helps to check the errors and to take the corrective action so that deviation from standards are minimized and stated goals of the organization are achieved in desired manner.According to modern concepts, _________ is a foreseeing action whereas earlier concept of _________ was used only when errors were detected. _________ in management means setting standards, measuring actual performance and taking corrective action.

a. Schedule of reinforcement
b. Turnover
c. Decision tree pruning
d. Control

8. The 'business case for _________', theorizes that in a global marketplace, a company that employs a diverse workforce (both men and women, people of many generations, people from ethnically and racially diverse backgrounds etc.) is better able to understand the demographics of the marketplace it serves and is thus better equipped to thrive in that marketplace than a company that has a more limited range of employee demographics.

An additional corollary suggests that a company that supports the _________ of its workforce can also improve employee satisfaction, productivity and retention.

a. Virtual team
b. Trademark
c. Diversity
d. Kanban

9. _________ is a contract between two parties, one being the employer and the other being the employee. An employee may be defined as: 'A person in the service of another under any contract of hire, express or implied, oral or written, where the employer has the power or right to control and direct the employee in the material details of how the work is to be performed.' Black's Law Dictionary page 471 (5th ed. 1979.)

a. Exit interview
b. Employment rate
c. Employment counsellor
d. Employment

10. The term _________ was created by President Lyndon B. Johnson when he signed Executive Order 11246 on September 24, 1965, created to prohibit federal contractors from discriminating against employees on the basis of race, sex, creed, religion, color, or national origin. In more recent times, most employers have also added sexual orientation to the list of non-discrimination.

The Executive Order also required contractors to implement affirmative action plans to increase the participation of minorities and women in the workplace.

a. A4e
b. A Stake in the Outcome
c. Equal Employment Opportunity
d. AAAI

11. The U.S. _________ is a federal agency whose goal is ending employment discrimination. The _________ investigates discrimination complaints based on an individual's race, color, national origin, religion, sex, age, disability and retaliation for reporting and/or opposing a discriminatory practice. The Commission is also tasked with filing suits on behalf of alleged victim(s) of discrimination against employers and as an adjudicatory for claims of discrimination brought against federal agencies.

a. Airbus SAS
b. ARCO
c. Airbus Industrie
d. Equal Employment Opportunity Commission

12. In economics, the term _________ refers to situations where the advancement of a qualified person within the hierarchy of an organization is stopped at a lower level because of some form of discrimination, most commonly sexism or racism, but since the term was coined, '_________' has also come to describe the limited advancement of the deaf, blind, disabled, aged and sexual minorities.It is an unofficial, invisible barrier that prevents women and minorities from advancing in businesses.

This situation is referred to as a 'ceiling' as there is a limitation blocking upward advancement, and 'glass' (transparent) because the limitation is not immediately apparent and is normally an unwritten and unofficial policy. This invisible barrier continues to exist, even though there are no explicit obstacles keeping minorities from acquiring advanced job positions - there are no advertisements that specifically say 'no minorities hired at this establishment', nor are there any formal orders that say 'minorities are not qualified' - but they do lie beneath the surface.

a. 33 Strategies of War
b. 1990 Clean Air Act
c. Glass Ceiling
d. 28-hour day

13. The _________ of 2002 (Pub.L. 107-204, 116 Stat. 745, enacted July 30, 2002), also known as the Public Company Accounting Reform and Investor Protection Act of 2002 and commonly called Sarbanes-Oxley, Sarbox or SOX, is a United States federal law enacted on July 30, 2002, as a reaction to a number of major corporate and accounting scandals including those affecting Enron, Tyco International, Adelphia, Peregrine Systems and WorldCom.

a. Fair Labor Standards Act
b. Sarbanes-Oxley Act of 2002
c. Letter of credit
d. Sarbanes-Oxley Act

14. The _________, also known as the Public Company Accounting Reform and Investor Protection Act of 2002 and commonly called Sarbanes-Oxley, Sarbox or SOX, is a United States federal law enacted on July 30, 2002, as a reaction to a number of major corporate and accounting scandals including those affecting Enron, Tyco International, Adelphia, Peregrine Systems and WorldCom.

a. Letter of credit
b. Munn v. Illinois
c. MacPherson v. Buick Motor Co.
d. Sarbanes-Oxley Act of 2002

15. _________ is unwelcome harassment of a sexual nature, or based upon the receiving party's sex or gender. In some contexts or circumstances, _________ may be illegal. It includes a range of behavior from seemingly mild transgressions and annoyances to actual sexual abuse or sexual assault.

a. 28-hour day
b. 1990 Clean Air Act
c. Hypernorms
d. Sexual harassment

16. _________ can be regarded as an outcome of mental processes (cognitive process) leading to the selection of a course of action among several alternatives. Every _________ process produces a final choice. The output can be an action or an opinion of choice.

a. 28-hour day
b. 33 Strategies of War
c. 1990 Clean Air Act
d. Decision making

17. A mutual shareholder or _________ is an individual or company (including a corporation) that legally owns one or more shares of stock in a joint stock company. A company's shareholders collectively own that company. Thus, the typical goal of such companies is to enhance shareholder value.

a. Shareholder
b. 1990 Clean Air Act
c. Free riding
d. Stockholder

18. _________ is a broad label that refers to any individuals or households that use goods and services generated within the economy. The concept of a _________ is used in different contexts, so that the usage and significance of the term may vary.

Typically when business people and economists talk of _________s they are talking about person as _________, an aggregated commodity item with little individuality other than that expressed in the buy/not-buy decision.

a. 28-hour day
b. 33 Strategies of War
c. 1990 Clean Air Act
d. Consumer

19. _________ laws are designed to ensure fair competition and the free flow of truthful information in the marketplace. The laws are designed to prevent businesses that engage in fraud or specified unfair practices from gaining an advantage over competitors and may provide additional protection for the weak and unable to take care of themselves. _________ laws are a form of government regulation which protects the interests of consumers.

a. Sarbanes-Oxley Act
b. Comprehensive Environmental Response, Compensation, and Liability Act
c. Certificate of Incorporation
d. Consumer protection

20. The general definition of an _________ is an evaluation of a person, organization, system, process, project or product. _________s are performed to ascertain the validity and reliability of information; also to provide an assessment of a system's internal control. The goal of an _________ is to express an opinion on the person / organization/system (etc) in question, under evaluation based on work done on a test basis.

a. Audit committee
b. A Stake in the Outcome
c. Internal control
d. Audit

1. A _________ is a computer program typically used to provide some form of artificial intelligence, which consists primarily of a set of rules about behavior. These rules, termed productions, are a basic representation found useful in AI planning, expert systems and action selection. A _________ provides the mechanism necessary to execute productions in order to achieve some goal for the system.

a. 33 Strategies of War
b. 28-hour day
c. 1990 Clean Air Act
d. Production System

2. _________, a business term, is a measure of how products and services supplied by a company meet or surpass customer expectation. It is seen as a key performance indicator within business and is part of the four perspectives of a Balanced Scorecard.

In a competitive marketplace where businesses compete for customers, _________ is seen as a key differentiator and increasingly has become a key element of business strategy.

a. Horizontal integration
b. Foreign ownership
c. Customer satisfaction
d. Critical Success Factor

3. _________ is a business management strategy aimed at embedding awareness of quality in all organizational processes. _________ has been widely used in manufacturing, education, hospitals, call centers, government, and service industries, as well as NASA space and science programs.

As defined by the International Organization for Standardization (ISO):

> '_________ is a management approach for an organization, centered on quality, based on the participation of all its members and aiming at long-term success through customer satisfaction, and benefits to all members of the organization and to society.' ISO 8402:1994

One major aim is to reduce variation from every process so that greater consistency of effort is obtained. (Royse, D., Thyer, B., Padgett D., ' Logan T., 2006)

a. 1990 Clean Air Act
b. Quality management
c. Total quality management
d. 28-hour day

4. _________ is a 'method to transform user demands into design quality, to deploy the functions forming quality, and to deploy methods for achieving the design quality into subsystems and component parts, and ultimately to specific elements of the manufacturing process.' , as described by Dr. Yoji Akao, who originally developed _________ in Japan in 1966, when the author combined his work in quality assurance and quality control points with function deployment used in Value Engineering.

_________ is designed to help planners focus on characteristics of a new or existing product or service from the viewpoints of market segments, company, or technology-development needs. The technique yields graphs and matrices.

a. 1990 Clean Air Act
b. Learning organization
c. Quality function deployment
d. Hoshin Kanri

5. _________ is an advertisement in which a particular product specifically mentions a competitor by name for the express purpose of showing why the competitor is inferior to the product naming it.

This should not be confused with parody advertisements, where a fictional product is being advertised for the purpose of poking fun at the particular advertisement, nor should it be confused with the use of a coined brand name for the purpose of comparing the product without actually naming an actual competitor. ('Wikipedia tastes better and is less filling than the Encyclopedia Galactica.')

In the 1980s, during what has been referred to as the cola wars, soft-drink manufacturer Pepsi ran a series of advertisements where people, caught on hidden camera, in a blind taste test, chose Pepsi over rival Coca-Cola.

a. 28-hour day
b. Comparative advertising
c. 33 Strategies of War
d. 1990 Clean Air Act

6. In economics, business, retail, and accounting, a _________ is the value of money that has been used up to produce something, and hence is not available for use anymore. In economics, a _________ is an alternative that is given up as a result of a decision. In business, the _________ may be one of acquisition, in which case the amount of money expended to acquire it is counted as _________.

a. Fixed costs
b. Cost overrun
c. Cost
d. Cost allocation

7. _________ is the state or fact of exclusive rights and control over property, which may be an object, land/real estate or intellectual property. An _________ right is also referred to as title. The concept of _________ has existed for thousands of years and in all cultures.

a. Emanation of the state
b. A Stake in the Outcome
c. A4e
d. Ownership

8. In economics, and cost accounting, _________ describes the total economic cost of production and is made up of variable costs, which vary according to the quantity of a good produced and include inputs such as labor and raw materials, plus fixed costs, which are independent of the quantity of a good produced and include inputs (capital) that cannot be varied in the short term, such as buildings and machinery. _________ in economics includes the total opportunity cost of each factor of production in addition to fixed and variable costs.

The rate at which _________ changes as the amount produced changes is called marginal cost.

a. Total Cost
b. 33 Strategies of War
c. 1990 Clean Air Act
d. 28-hour day

9. _________ is a financial estimate designed to help consumers and enterprise managers assess direct and indirect costs It is a form of full cost accounting.

a. 28-hour day
b. Total Cost of Ownership
c. 33 Strategies of War
d. 1990 Clean Air Act

10. _________ is one of the managerial functions like planning, organizing, staffing and directing. It is an important function because it helps to check the errors and to take the corrective action so that deviation from standards are minimized and stated goals of the organization are achieved in desired manner.According to modern concepts, _________ is a foreseeing action whereas earlier concept of _________ was used only when errors were detected. _________ in management means setting standards, measuring actual performance and taking corrective action.

a. Control
b. Turnover
c. Decision tree pruning
d. Schedule of reinforcement

11. In engineering and manufacturing, _________ and quality engineering are used in developing systems to ensure products or services are designed and produced to meet or exceed customer requirements. Refer to the definition by Merriam-Webster for further information . These systems are often developed in conjunction with other business and engineering disciplines using a cross-functional approach.

a. Process capability
b. Quality control
c. Statistical process control
d. Single Minute Exchange of Die

12. _________ refers to metrics and measures of output from production processes, per unit of input. Labor _________, for example, is typically measured as a ratio of output per labor-hour, an input. _________ may be conceived of as a metrics of the technical or engineering efficiency of production.

a. Remanufacturing
b. Productivity
c. Value engineering
d. Master production schedule

13. _________ or lean production, which is often known simply as 'Lean', is a production practice that considers the expenditure of resources for any goal other than the creation of value for the end customer to be wasteful, and thus a target for elimination. Working from the perspective of the customer who consumes a product or service, 'value' is defined as any action or process that a customer would be willing to pay for. Basically, lean is centered around creating more value with less work.

a. Theory of constraints
b. Lean Manufacturing
c. Six Sigma
d. Production line

14. _________ is the temporary suspension or permanent termination of employment of an employee or (more commonly) a group of employees for business reasons, such as the decision that certain positions are no longer necessary or a business slow-down or interruption in work. Originally the term '_________' referred exclusively to a temporary interruption in work, as when factory work cyclically falls off. However, in recent times the term can also refer to the permanent elimination of a position.

a. Layoff
b. Wrongful dismissal
c. Termination of employment
d. Retirement

15. A _________ or business method is a collection of related, structured activities or tasks that produce a specific service or product (serve a particular goal) for a particular customer or customers. It often can be visualized with a flowchart as a sequence of activities.

There are three types of _________es:

1. Management processes, the processes that govern the operation of a system. Typical management processes include 'Corporate Governance' and 'Strategic Management'.
2. Operational processes, processes that constitute the core business and create the primary value stream. Typical operational processes are Purchasing, Manufacturing, Marketing, and Sales.
3. Supporting processes, which support the core processes. Examples include Accounting, Recruitment, Technical support.

A _________ begins with a customer's need and ends with a customer's need fulfillment. Process oriented organizations break down the barriers of structural departments and try to avoid functional silos.

a. 28-hour day
b. 33 Strategies of War
c. 1990 Clean Air Act
d. Business process

16. _________ is, in computer science and management, an approach aiming at improvements by means of elevating efficiency and effectiveness of the business process that exist within and across organizations. The key to _________ is for organizations to look at their business processes from a 'clean slate' perspective and determine how they can best construct these processes to improve how they conduct business. _________ Cycle.

_________ is also known as _________, Business Process Redesign, Business Transformation, or Business Process Change Management.

a. Product life cycle
b. Business process reengineering
c. Personal management interview
d. Horizontal integration

17. The _________ of 1938 (_________, ch. 676, 52 Stat. 1060, June 25, 1938, 29 U.S.C. ch.8), also called the Wages and Hours Bill, is United States federal law that applies to employees engaged in interstate commerce or employed by an enterprise engaged in commerce or in the production of goods for commerce, unless the employer can claim an exemption from coverage. The _________ established a national minimum wage, guaranteed time and a half for overtime in certain jobs, and prohibited most employment of minors in 'oppressive child labor,' a term defined in the statute.

a. Family and Medical Leave Act of 1993
b. Fair Labor Standards Act
c. Board of directors
d. Joint venture

18. _________ are conventions, treaties and recommendations designed to eliminate unjust and inhumane labour practices. The primary inernational agency charged with developing such standards is the International Labour Organization (ILO.) Established in 1919, the ILO advocates international standards as essential for the eradication of labour conditions involving 'injustice, hardship and privation'.

a. Airbus SAS
b. International labour standards
c. Airbus Industrie
d. Anaconda Copper

19. _________ is a management technique pioneered by Michael Phillips in San Francisco in the late '60's and early '70s. The concept's most visible success was by Jack Stack and his team at SRC Holdings and popularized in 1995 by John Case. The technique is to give employees all relevant financial information about the company so they can make better decisions as workers.

a. A4e
b. A Stake in the Outcome
c. Open-book management
d. AAAI

20. In game theory, an _________ is a set of moves or strategies taken by the players, or their payoffs resulting from the actions or strategies taken by all players. The two are complementary in that given knowledge of the set of strategies of all players, the final state of the game is known, as are any relevant payoffs. In a game where chance or a random event is involved, the _________ is not known from only the set of strategies, but is only realized when the random event(s) are realized.
a. A Stake in the Outcome
b. A4e
c. AAAI
d. Outcome

21. _________ is the process of disassembly and recovery at the module level and, eventually, at the component level. It requires the repair or replacement of worn out or obsolete components and modules. Parts subject to degradation affecting the performance or the expected life of the whole are replaced.
a. Methods-time measurement
b. Capacity planning
c. Productivity
d. ReManufacturing

22. _________ refers to increasing the spiritual, political, social or economic strength of individuals and communities. It often involves the empowered developing confidence in their own capacities.

The term Human _________ covers a vast landscape of meanings, interpretations, definitions and disciplines ranging from psychology and philosophy to the highly commercialized Self-Help industry and Motivational sciences.

a. A Stake in the Outcome
b. A4e
c. Empowerment
d. AAAI

23. In organizational development (OD), _________ is a series of actions taken by a Process Owner to identify, analyze and improve existing processes within an organization to meet new goals and objectives. These actions often follow a specific methodology or strategy to create successful results. A sampling of these are listed below.
a. Supervisory board
b. Letter of resignation
c. Process improvement
d. Product innovation

24. _________ refers to the movement of cash into or out of a business or financial product. It is usually measured during a specified, finite period of time. Measurement of _________ can be used

- to determine a project's rate of return or value. The time of _________s into and out of projects are used as inputs in financial models such as internal rate of return, and net present value.
- to determine problems with a business's liquidity. Being profitable does not necessarily mean being liquid. A company can fail because of a shortage of cash, even while profitable.
- as an alternate measure of a business's profits when it is believed that accrual accounting concepts do not represent economic realities. For example, a company may be notionally profitable but generating little operational cash (as may be the case for a company that barters its products rather than selling for cash.) In such a case, the company may be deriving additional operating cash by issuing shares evaluating default risk, re-investment requirements, etc.

_________ is a generic term used differently depending on the context. It may be defined by users for their own purposes.

a. Cash flow
b. Sweat equity
c. Gross profit
d. Gross profit margin

25. Quality management can be considered to have three main components: quality control, quality assurance and _________. Quality management is focused not only on product quality, but also the means to achieve it. Quality management therefore uses quality assurance and control of processes as well as products to achieve more consistent quality.

a. Quality management
b. 1990 Clean Air Act
c. 28-hour day
d. Quality improvement

26. The general definition of an _________ is an evaluation of a person, organization, system, process, project or product. _________s are performed to ascertain the validity and reliability of information; also to provide an assessment of a system's internal control. The goal of an _________ is to express an opinion on the person / organization/system (etc) in question, under evaluation based on work done on a test basis.

a. A Stake in the Outcome
b. Audit
c. Audit committee
d. Internal control

27. _________ is an inventory strategy that strives to improve the return on investment of a business by reducing in-process inventory and its associated carrying costs. To meet _________ objectives, the process relies on signals between different points in the process. This means the process is often driven by a series of signals, or Kanban , which tell production when to make the next part. Kanban are usually 'tickets' but can be simple visual signals, such as the presence or absence of a part on a shelf. Implemented correctly, _________ can dramatically improve a manufacturing organization's return on investment, quality, and efficiency.

a. 33 Strategies of War
b. 28-hour day
c. 1990 Clean Air Act
d. Just-in-time

28. The _________ in statistical process control is a tool used to determine whether a manufacturing or business process is in a state of statistical control or not.

If the chart indicates that the process is currently under control then it can be used with confidence to predict the future performance of the process. If the chart indicates that the process being monitored is not in control, the pattern it reveals can help determine the source of variation to be eliminated to bring the process back into control.

a. Control chart
b. Failure rate
c. Time series analysis
d. Simple moving average

29. A _________ is a volunteer group composed of workers (or even students), usually under the leadership of their supervisor (but they can elect a team leader), who are trained to identify, analyse and solve work-related problems and present their solutions to management in order to improve the performance of the organization, and motivate and enrich the work of employees. When matured, true _________s become self-managing, having gained the confidence of management. _________s are an alternative to the dehumanising concept of the Division of Labour, where workers or individuals are treated like robots.

a. Competency-based job descriptions
b. Connectionist expert systems
c. Certified in Production and Inventory Management
d. Quality circle

1. _________ is a process of gathering, analyzing, and dispensing information for tactical or strategic purposes. The _________ process entails obtaining both factual and subjective information on the business environments in which a company is operating or considering entering.

There are three ways of scanning the business environment:

- Ad-hoc scanning - Short term, infrequent examinations usually initiated by a crisis
- Regular scanning - Studies done on a regular schedule (say, once a year)
- Continuous scanning(also called continuous learning) - continuous structured data collection and processing on a broad range of environmental factors

Most commentators feel that in today's turbulent business environment the best scanning method available is continuous scanning. This allows the firm to :

-act quickly-take advantage of opportunities before competitors do-respond to environmental threats before significant damage is done

a. Environmental scanning
b. AAAI
c. A Stake in the Outcome
d. A4e

2. A _________ is a brief written statement of the purpose of a company or organization. Ideally, a _________ guides the actions of the organization, spells out its overall goal, provides a sense of direction, and guides decision making for all levels of management.

_________s often contain the following:

- Purpose and aim of the organization
- The organization's primary stakeholders: clients, stockholders, etc.
- Responsibilities of the organization toward these stakeholders
- Products and services offered

In developing a _________:

- Encourage as much input as feasible from employees, volunteers, and other stakeholders
- Publicize it broadly

The _________ can be used to resolve differences between business stakeholders. Stakeholders include: employees including managers and executives, stockholders, board of directors, customers, suppliers, distributors, creditors, governments (local, state, federal, etc.), unions, competitors, NGO's, and the general public.

a. Mission statement
b. 1990 Clean Air Act
c. 28-hour day
d. 33 Strategies of War

3. The _________ of 1938 (_________, ch. 676, 52 Stat. 1060, June 25, 1938, 29 U.S.C. ch.8), also called the Wages and Hours Bill, is United States federal law that applies to employees engaged in interstate commerce or employed by an enterprise engaged in commerce or in the production of goods for commerce, unless the employer can claim an exemption from coverage. The _________ established a national minimum wage, guaranteed time and a half for overtime in certain jobs, and prohibited most employment of minors in 'oppressive child labor,' a term defined in the statute.

a. Board of directors
b. Family and Medical Leave Act of 1993
c. Joint venture
d. Fair Labor Standards Act

4. _________ are conventions, treaties and recommendations designed to eliminate unjust and inhumane labour practices. The primary inernational agency charged with developing such standards is the International Labour Organization (ILO.) Established in 1919, the ILO advocates international standards as essential for the eradication of labour conditions involving 'injustice, hardship and privation'.

a. Anaconda Copper
b. International labour standards
c. Airbus Industric
d. Airbus SAS

5. _________ is something that a firm can do well and that meets the following three conditions:

Competencies are things that companys execute well across several business units or product sectors.

Firms usually have few competencies, but these are usually less liable to change rapidly.

1. It provides consumer benefits
2. It is not easy for competitors to imitate
3. It can be leveraged widely to many products and markets.

A _________ can take various forms, including technical/subject matter know-how, a reliable process and/or close relationships with customers and suppliers (Mascarenhas et al. 1998.)

a. Learning-by-doing
b. NAIRU
c. Dominant Design
d. Core competency

6. The term _________ collectively refers to all resources that determine the value and the competitiveness of an enterprise. As such, it includes as subsets the attributes that concur to building all financial statements as well as the balance sheet.

a. AAAI
b. A4e
c. A Stake in the Outcome
d. Intellectual capital

7. _________ comprises a range of practices used in an organisation to identify, create, represent, distribute and enable adoption of insights and experiences. Such insights and experiences comprise knowledge, either embodied in individuals or embedded in organisational processes or practice.

An established discipline since 1991 , _________ includes courses taught in the fields of business administration, information systems, management, and library and information sciences .

a. 1990 Clean Air Act
b. 33 Strategies of War
c. Knowledge management
d. 28-hour day

8. _________ is an idea in the field of Organizational studies and management which describes the psychology, attitudes, experiences, beliefs and Values (personal and cultural values) of an organization. It has been defined as 'the specific collection of values and norms that are shared by people and groups in an organization and that control the way they interact with each other and with stakeholders outside the organization.'

This definition continues to explain organizational values also known as 'beliefs and ideas about what kinds of goals members of an organization should pursue and ideas about the appropriate kinds or standards of behavior organizational members should use to achieve these goals. From organizational values develop organizational norms, guidelines or expectations that prescribe appropriate kinds of behavior by employees in particular situations and control the behavior of organizational members towards one another.'

_________ is not the same as corporate culture.

a. Organizational effectiveness
b. Union shop
c. Organizational culture
d. Organizational development

9. _________ has been described as the 'process of social influence in which one person can enlist the aid and support of others in the accomplishment of a common task' . A definition more inclusive of followers comes from Alan Keith of Genentech who said '_________ is ultimately about creating a way for people to contribute to making something extraordinary happen.'

_________ is one of the most salient aspects of the organizational context. However, defining _________ has been challenging.

a. 28-hour day
b. 1990 Clean Air Act
c. Situational leadership
d. Leadership

10. In sociology, anthropology and cultural studies, a _________ is a group of people with a culture (whether distinct or hidden) which differentiates them from the larger culture to which they belong. If a particular _________ is characterized by a systematic opposition to the dominant culture, it may be described as a counterculture.

As early as 1950, David Riesman distinguished between a majority, 'which passively accepted commercially provided styles and meanings, and a '_________' which actively sought a minority style ...

a. 28-hour day
b. 1990 Clean Air Act
c. 33 Strategies of War
d. Subculture

11. A _________ is a contemporary apporach to organizational design. It is an organization that is not defined by, or limited to, the horizontal, vertical, or external boundaries imposed by a predefined structure. This term was coined by former GE chairman Jack Welch because he wanted to eliminate vertical and horizontal boundaries within GE and break down external barriers between the company and its customers and suppliers.

a. Headquarters
b. Boundaryless organization
c. Chief risk officer
d. Business Roundtable

12. An _________ is a mostly hierarchical concept of subordination of entities that collaborate and contribute to serve one common aim.

Organizations are a variant of clustered entities. The structure of an organization is usually set up in many a styles, dependent on their objectives and ambience.

a. Organizational development
b. Open shop
c. Informal organization
d. Organizational structure

13. The _________ 1970 is an Act of the United Kingdom Parliament which prohibits any less favourable treatment between men and women in terms of pay and conditions of employment. It came into force on 29 December 1975. The term pay is interpreted in a broad sense to include, on top of wages, things like holidays, pension rights, company perks and some kinds of bonuses.
a. Architectural Barriers Act of 1968
b. Australian labour law
c. Oncale v. Sundowner Offshore Services
d. Equal Pay Act

14. The _________ was a period in the late 18th and early 19th centuries when major changes in agriculture, manufacturing, mining, and transportation had a profound effect on the socioeconomic and cultural conditions in Britain. The changes subsequently spread throughout Europe, North America, and eventually the world. The onset of the _________ marked a major turning point in human society; almost every aspect of daily life was eventually influenced in some way.
a. Abraham Harold Maslow
b. Industrial Revolution
c. Affiliation
d. Adam Smith

15. _________ can be regarded as an outcome of mental processes (cognitive process) leading to the selection of a course of action among several alternatives. Every _________ process produces a final choice. The output can be an action or an opinion of choice.
a. Decision making
b. 33 Strategies of War
c. 1990 Clean Air Act
d. 28-hour day

16. A _________ is a type of business entity in which partners (owners) share with each other the profits or losses of the business. _________s are often favored over corporations for taxation purposes, as the _________ structure does not generally incur a tax on profits before it is distributed to the partners (i.e. there is no dividend tax levied.) However, depending on the _________ structure and the jurisdiction in which it operates, owners of a _________ may be exposed to greater personal liability than they would as shareholders of a corporation.
a. Mediation
b. Partnership
c. Federal Employers Liability Act
d. Due process

17. A mutual shareholder or _________ is an individual or company (including a corporation) that legally owns one or more shares of stock in a joint stock company. A company's shareholders collectively own that company. Thus, the typical goal of such companies is to enhance shareholder value.
a. Shareholder
b. Free riding
c. 1990 Clean Air Act
d. Stockholder

18. While the full name of the Swiss verein is Deloitte Touche Tohmatsu, in 1989 it initially branded itself _________ and then simply Deloitte. In 2003 the rebranding campaign was commissioned by Bill Parrett, the then CEO of DTT, and led by Jerry Leamon, the global Clients and Markets leader.

Deloitte member firms offer services in the following functions, with country-specific variations on their legal implementation (i.e. all operating within a single company or through separate legal entities operating as subsidiaries of an umbrella legal entity for the country.)

a. Deloitte ' Touche
b. 33 Strategies of War
c. 1990 Clean Air Act
d. 28-hour day

19. In economics, the people in the _________ are the suppliers of labor. The _________ is all the nonmilitary people who are employed or unemployed. In 2005, the worldwide _________ was over 3 billion people.
a. Labor force
b. Decent work
c. Departmentalization
d. Pink-collar worker

20. _________ is the strategic and coherent approach to the management of an organisation's most valued assets - the people working there who individually and collectively contribute to the achievement of the objectives of the business. The terms '_________' and 'human resources' (HR) have largely replaced the term 'personnel management' as a description of the processes involved in managing people in organizations. In simple sense, _________ means employing people, developing their resources, utilizing, maintaining and compensating their services in tune with the job and organizational requirement.
a. Job knowledge
b. Human Resource Management
c. Progressive discipline
d. Revolving door syndrome

21. _________ or lean production, which is often known simply as 'Lean', is a production practice that considers the expenditure of resources for any goal other than the creation of value for the end customer to be wasteful, and thus a target for elimination. Working from the perspective of the customer who consumes a product or service, 'value' is defined as any action or process that a customer would be willing to pay for. Basically, lean is centered around creating more value with less work.
a. Six Sigma
b. Lean Manufacturing
c. Theory of constraints
d. Production line

22. _________ is a contract between two parties, one being the employer and the other being the employee. An employee may be defined as: 'A person in the service of another under any contract of hire, express or implied, oral or written, where the employer has the power or right to control and direct the employee in the material details of how the work is to be performed.' Black's Law Dictionary page 471 (5th ed. 1979.)
a. Exit interview
b. Employment
c. Employment counsellor
d. Employment rate

23. _________ is the largest book retailer in the United States, operating mainly through its Barnes ' Noble Booksellers chain of bookstores headquartered in lower Fifth Avenue in Manhattan.

The company operates the chain of small 'B.

a. 1990 Clean Air Act
b. 28-hour day
c. 33 Strategies of War
d. Barnes ' Noble, Inc.

24. _________, commonly known as e-commerce, consists of the buying and selling of products or services over electronic systems such as the Internet and other computer networks. The amount of trade conducted electronically has grown extraordinarily with widespread Internet usage. The use of commerce is conducted in this way, spurring and drawing on innovations in electronic funds transfer, supply chain management, Internet marketing, online transaction processing, electronic data interchange (EDI), inventory management systems, and automated data collection systems.

a. Online shopping
b. A4e
c. A Stake in the Outcome
d. Electronic commerce

1. _________ is an organization's process of defining its strategy and making decisions on allocating its resources to pursue this strategy, including its capital and people. Various business analysis techniques can be used in _________, including SWOT analysis (Strengths, Weaknesses, Opportunities, and Threats) and PEST analysis (Political, Economic, Social, and Technological analysis) or STEER analysis involving Socio-cultural, Technological, Economic, Ecological, and Regulatory factors and EPISTEL (Environment, Political, Informatic, Social, Technological, Economic and Legal)

_________ is the formal consideration of an organization's future course. All _________ deals with at least one of three key questions:

1. 'What do we do?'
2. 'For whom do we do it?'
3. 'How do we excel?'

In business _________, the third question is better phrased 'How can we beat or avoid competition?'. (Bradford and Duncan, page 1.)

a. Strategic planning
b. 28-hour day
c. 1990 Clean Air Act
d. 33 Strategies of War

2. A _________ is a brief written statement of the purpose of a company or organization. Ideally, a _________ guides the actions of the organization, spells out its overall goal, provides a sense of direction, and guides decision making for all levels of management.

_________s often contain the following:

- Purpose and aim of the organization
- The organization's primary stakeholders: clients, stockholders, etc.
- Responsibilities of the organization toward these stakeholders
- Products and services offered

In developing a _________:

- Encourage as much input as feasible from employees, volunteers, and other stakeholders
- Publicize it broadly

The _________ can be used to resolve differences between business stakeholders. Stakeholders include: employees including managers and executives, stockholders, board of directors, customers, suppliers, distributors, creditors, governments (local, state, federal, etc.), unions, competitors, NGO's, and the general public.

a. 33 Strategies of War
b. 1990 Clean Air Act
c. 28-hour day
d. Mission statement

3. _________ was a writer, management consultant, and self-described 'social ecologist.' Widely considered to be 'the father of modern management,' his 39 books and countless scholarly and popular articles explored how humans are organized across all sectors of society--in business, government and the nonprofit world. His writings have predicted many of the major developments of the late twentieth century, including privatization and decentralization; the rise of Japan to economic world power; the decisive importance of marketing; and the emergence of the information society with its necessity of lifelong learning. In 1959, Drucker coined the term 'knowledge worker' and later in his life considered knowledge work productivity to be the next frontier of management.

a. Peter Ferdinand Drucker
b. Debora L. Spar
c. Chrissie Hynde
d. Jacques Al-Salawat Nasruddin Nasser

4. The U.S. _________ is a federal agency whose goal is ending employment discrimination. The _________ investigates discrimination complaints based on an individual's race, color, national origin, religion, sex, age, disability and retaliation for reporting and/or opposing a discriminatory practice. The Commission is also tasked with filing suits on behalf of alleged victim(s) of discrimination against employers and as an adjudicatory for claims of discrimination brought against federal agencies.

a. Equal Employment Opportunity Commission
b. ARCO
c. Airbus Industrie
d. Airbus SAS

5. _________ generally refers to a list of all planned expenses and revenues. It is a plan for saving and spending. A _________ is an important concept in microeconomics, which uses a _________ line to illustrate the trade-offs between two or more goods.

a. 1990 Clean Air Act
b. Budget
c. 33 Strategies of War
d. 28-hour day

6. _________ is a contract between two parties, one being the employer and the other being the employee. An employee may be defined as: 'A person in the service of another under any contract of hire, express or implied, oral or written, where the employer has the power or right to control and direct the employee in the material details of how the work is to be performed.' Black's Law Dictionary page 471 (5th ed. 1979.)

a. Employment
b. Employment rate
c. Exit interview
d. Employment counsellor

7. The term _________ was created by President Lyndon B. Johnson when he signed Executive Order 11246 on September 24, 1965, created to prohibit federal contractors from discriminating against employees on the basis of race, sex, creed, religion, color, or national origin. In more recent times, most employers have also added sexual orientation to the list of non-discrimination.

The Executive Order also required contractors to implement affirmative action plans to increase the participation of minorities and women in the workplace.

a. A4e
b. AAAI
c. A Stake in the Outcome
d. Equal Employment Opportunity

8. _________ can be regarded as an outcome of mental processes (cognitive process) leading to the selection of a course of action among several alternatives. Every _________ process produces a final choice. The output can be an action or an opinion of choice.

a. 1990 Clean Air Act
b. Decision making
c. 33 Strategies of War
d. 28-hour day

9. _________ is an increasingly broadening term with which an organization, or other human system describes the combination of traditionally administrative personnel functions with acquisition and application of skills, knowledge and experience, Employee Relations and resource planning at various levels. The field draws upon concepts developed in Industrial/Organizational Psychology and System Theory. _________ has at least two related interpretations depending on context. The original usage derives from political economy and economics, where it was traditionally called labor, one of four factors of production although this perspective is changing as a function of new and ongoing research into more strategic approaches at national levels. This first usage is used more in terms of '_________ development', and can go beyond just organizations to the level of nations . The more traditional usage within corporations and businesses refers to the individuals within a firm or agency, and to the portion of the organization that deals with hiring, firing, training, and other personnel issues, typically referred to as `_________ management'.

a. Human resources
b. Progressive discipline
c. Human resource management
d. Bradford Factor

10. A _________ is typically described as a deliberate plan of action to guide decisions and achieve rational outcome(s.) However, the term may also be used to denote what is actually done, even though it is unplanned.

The term may apply to government, private sector organizations and groups, and individuals.

a. 1990 Clean Air Act
b. 28-hour day
c. Policy
d. 33 Strategies of War

11. _________ is the temporary suspension or permanent termination of employment of an employee or (more commonly) a group of employees for business reasons, such as the decision that certain positions are no longer necessary or a business slow-down or interruption in work. Originally the term '_________' referred exclusively to a temporary interruption in work, as when factory work cyclically falls off. However, in recent times the term can also refer to the permanent elimination of a position.

a. Retirement
b. Layoff
c. Wrongful dismissal
d. Termination of employment

12. A _________ is a plan devised for a specific situation when things could go wrong. _________s are often devised by governments or businesses who want to be prepared for anything that could happen. They are sometimes known as 'Back-up plans', 'Worst-case scenario plans' or 'Plan B'.

a. 28-hour day
b. 33 Strategies of War
c. 1990 Clean Air Act
d. Contingency plan

13. _________ is a term that refers both to:

- a formal discipline used to help appraise, or assess, the case for a project or proposal, which itself is a process known as project appraisal; and
- an informal approach to making decisions of any kind.

Under both definitions the process involves, whether explicitly or implicitly, weighing the total expected costs against the total expected benefits of one or more actions in order to choose the best or most profitable option. The formal process is often referred to as either CBA (_________) or BCost-benefit analysis

A hallmark of CBA is that all benefits and all costs are expressed in money terms, and are adjusted for the time value of money, so that all flows of benefits and flows of project costs over time (which tend to occur at different points in time) are expressed on a common basis in terms of their 'present value.' Closely related, but slightly different, formal techniques include Cost-effectiveness analysis, Economic impact analysis, Fiscal impact analysis and Social Return on Investment(SROI) analysis. The latter builds upon the logic of _________, but differs in that it is explicitly designed to inform the practical decision-making of enterprise managers and investors focused on optimising their social and environmental impacts.

a. Cost-benefit analysis
b. Gittins index
c. Kepner-Tregoe
d. Decision engineering

14. _________ is the process of estimation in unknown situations. Prediction is a similar, but more general term. Both can refer to estimation of time series, cross-sectional or longitudinal data.

a. 33 Strategies of War
b. 1990 Clean Air Act
c. 28-hour day
d. Forecasting

15. _________ is a process of agreeing upon objectives within an organization so that management and employees agree to the objectives and understand what they are in the organization.

The term '_________' was first popularized by Peter Drucker in his 1954 book 'The Practice of Management'.

The essence of _________ is participative goal setting, choosing course of actions and decision making.

a. Clean sheet review
b. Business economics
c. Job enrichment
d. Management by objectives

16. In mathematics, _________ is a technique for optimization of a linear objective function, subject to linear equality and linear inequality constraints. Informally, _________ determines the way to achieve the best outcome (such as maximum profit or lowest cost) in a given mathematical model and given some list of requirements represented as linear equations.

More formally, given a polytope (for example, a polygon or a polyhedron), and a real-valued affine function

$$f(x_1, x_2, \dots, x_n) = c_1 x_1 + c_2 x_2 + \cdots + c_n x_n + d$$

defined on this polytope, a _________ method will find a point in the polytope where this function has the smallest (or largest) value.

a. Linear programming
b. 1990 Clean Air Act
c. Slack variable
d. Linear programming relaxation

17. The _________ was a period in the late 18th and early 19th centuries when major changes in agriculture, manufacturing, mining, and transportation had a profound effect on the socioeconomic and cultural conditions in Britain. The changes subsequently spread throughout Europe, North America, and eventually the world. The onset of the _________ marked a major turning point in human society; almost every aspect of daily life was eventually influenced in some way.

a. Abraham Harold Maslow
b. Industrial Revolution
c. Affiliation
d. Adam Smith

18. _________ is, in very basic words, a position a firm occupies against its competitors.

According to Michael Porter, the three methods for creating a sustainable _________ are through:

1. Cost leadership

2. Differentiation

3. Focus (economics)

a. Theory Z
b. 1990 Clean Air Act
c. 28-hour day
d. Competitive advantage

19. _________ is something that a firm can do well and that meets the following three conditions:

Competencies are things that companys execute well across several business units or product sectors.

Firms usually have few competencies, but these are usually less liable to change rapidly.

1. It provides consumer benefits
2. It is not easy for competitors to imitate
3. It can be leveraged widely to many products and markets.

A _________ can take various forms, including technical/subject matter know-how, a reliable process and/or close relationships with customers and suppliers (Mascarenhas et al. 1998.)

a. Learning-by-doing
b. Core competency
c. NAIRU
d. Dominant Design

20. _________ is the term used to describe a situation where different entities cooperate advantageously for a final outcome. Simply defined, it means that the whole is greater than the sum of the individual parts. Although the whole will be greater than each individual part, this is not the concept of _________.

a. 28-hour day
b. 33 Strategies of War
c. 1990 Clean Air Act
d. Synergy

21. _________ is a form of applied ethics that examines ethical principles and moral or ethical problems that arise in a business environment. It applies to all aspects of business conduct and is relevant to the conduct of individuals and business organizations as a whole. Applied ethics is a field of ethics that deals with ethical questions in many fields such as medical, technical, legal and _________.

a. Business ethics
b. Facilitation payments
c. Corporate Sustainability
d. Hypernorms

22. _________ is one of the managerial functions like planning, organizing, staffing and directing. It is an important function because it helps to check the errors and to take the corrective action so that deviation from standards are minimized and stated goals of the organization are achieved in desired manner.According to modern concepts, _________ is a foreseeing action whereas earlier concept of _________ was used only when errors were detected. _________ in management means setting standards, measuring actual performance and taking corrective action.

a. Decision tree pruning
b. Turnover
c. Control
d. Schedule of reinforcement

23. In microeconomics and strategic management, the term _________ describes a type of ownership and control. It is a strategy used by a business or corporation that seeks to sell a type of product in numerous markets. _________ in marketing is much more common than vertical integration is in production.

a. Career development
b. No-bid contract
c. Horizontal integration
d. Farmshoring

24. In microeconomics and management, the term _________ describes a style of management control. Vertically integrated companies are united through a hierarchy with a common owner. Usually each member of the hierarchy produces a different product or (market-specific) service, and the products combine to satisfy a common need.

a. 1990 Clean Air Act
b. 33 Strategies of War
c. Vertical integration
d. 28-hour day

25. A _________ is a name or trademark connected with a product or producer. _________s have become increasingly important components of culture and the economy, now being described as 'cultural accessories and personal philosophies'.

Some people distinguish the psychological aspect of a _________ from the experiential aspect.

a. Brand
b. Brand loyalty
c. Brand extension
d. Brand awareness

26. _________ is a business management strategy aimed at embedding awareness of quality in all organizational processes. _________ has been widely used in manufacturing, education, hospitals, call centers, government, and service industries, as well as NASA space and science programs.

As defined by the International Organization for Standardization (ISO):

> '_________ is a management approach for an organization, centered on quality, based on the participation of all its members and aiming at long-term success through customer satisfaction, and benefits to all members of the organization and to society.' ISO 8402:1994

One major aim is to reduce variation from every process so that greater consistency of effort is obtained. (Royse, D., Thyer, B., Padgett D., ' Logan T., 2006)

a. Quality management
b. 28-hour day
c. 1990 Clean Air Act
d. Total quality management

27. In business, a _________ is a product or a business unit that generates unusually high profit margins: so high that it is responsible for a large amount of a company's operating profit. This profit far exceeds the amount necessary to maintain the _________ business, and the excess is used by the business for other purposes.

A firm is said to be acting as a _________ when its earnings per share (EPS) is equal to its dividends per share (DPS), or in other words, when a firm pays out 100% of its free cash flow (FCF) to its shareholders as dividends at the end of each accounting term.

a. Cash cow
b. Design management in organization
c. Workflow
d. Middle management

28. The _________ (Situation, Task, Action, Result) format is a job interview technique used by interviewers to gather all the relevant information about a specific capability that the job requires. This interview format is said to have a higher degree of predictability of future on-the-job performance than the traditional interview.

- Situation: The interviewer wants you to present a recent challenge and situation in which you found yourself.
- Task: What did you have to achieve? The interviewer will be looking to see what you were trying to achieve from the situation.
- Action: What did you do? The interviewer will be looking for information on what you did, why you did it and what were the alternatives.
- Results: What was the outcome of your actions? What did you achieve through your actions and did you meet your objectives. What did you learn from this experience and have you used this learning since?

.

a. Competency-based job descriptions
b. Rasch models
c. Phrase completion
d. Star

29. _________ is an integrated communications-based process through which individuals and communities discover that existing and newly-identified needs and wants may be satisfied by the products and services of others.

_________ is defined by the American _________ Association as the activity, set of institutions, and processes for creating, communicating, delivering, and exchanging offerings that have value for customers, clients, partners, and society at large. The term developed from the original meaning which referred literally to going to market, as in shopping, or going to a market to buy or sell goods or services.

a. Customer relationship management
b. Market development
c. Disruptive technology
d. Marketing

30. A _________ is a process that can allow an organization to concentrate its limited resources on the greatest opportunities to increase sales and achieve a sustainable competitive advantage. A _________ should be centered around the key concept that customer satisfaction is the main goal.

A _________ is a written plan which combines product development, promotion, distribution, and pricing approach, identifies the firm's marketing goals, and explains how they will be achieved within a stated timeframe.

a. Category management
b. Disruptive technology
c. Marketing strategy
d. Product bundling

31. The phrase _________, according to the Organization for Economic Co-operation and Development, refers to 'creative work undertaken on a systematic basis in order to increase the stock of knowledge, including knowledge of man, culture and society, and the use of this stock of knowledge to devise new applications [sic]'

New product design and development is more than often a crucial factor in the survival of a company. In an industry that is fast changing, firms must continually revise their design and range of products. This is necessary due to continuous technology change and development as well as other competitors and the changing preference of customers.

a. 33 Strategies of War
b. 28-hour day
c. 1990 Clean Air Act
d. Research and development

1. _________ can be regarded as an outcome of mental processes (cognitive process) leading to the selection of a course of action among several alternatives. Every _________ process produces a final choice. The output can be an action or an opinion of choice.

a. Decision making | b. 33 Strategies of War
c. 28-hour day | d. 1990 Clean Air Act

2. A _________ is a list of the general tasks and responsibilities of a position. Typically, it also includes to whom the position reports, specifications such as the qualifications needed by the person in the job, salary range for the position, etc. A _________ is usually developed by conducting a job analysis, which includes examining the tasks and sequences of tasks necessary to perform the job.

a. Recruitment advertising | b. Recruitment
c. Recruitment Process Insourcing | d. Job description

3. _________ is one of the managerial functions like planning, organizing, staffing and directing. It is an important function because it helps to check the errors and to take the corrective action so that deviation from standards are minimized and stated goals of the organization are achieved in desired manner.According to modern concepts, _________ is a foreseeing action whereas earlier concept of _________ was used only when errors were detected. _________ in management means setting standards, measuring actual performance and taking corrective action.

a. Turnover | b. Schedule of reinforcement
c. Decision tree pruning | d. Control

4. A _________ is a framework for creating economic, social, and/or other forms of value. The term _________ is thus used for a broad range of informal and formal descriptions to represent core aspects of a business, including purpose, offerings, strategies, infrastructure, organizational structures, trading practices, and operational processes and policies.

Conceptualizations of _________s try to formalize informal descriptions into building blocks and their relationships.

a. Business networking | b. Gap analysis
c. Business model design | d. Business model

5. _________, commonly known as e-commerce, consists of the buying and selling of products or services over electronic systems such as the Internet and other computer networks. The amount of trade conducted electronically has grown extraordinarily with widespread Internet usage. The use of commerce is conducted in this way, spurring and drawing on innovations in electronic funds transfer, supply chain management, Internet marketing, online transaction processing, electronic data interchange (EDI), inventory management systems, and automated data collection systems.

a. A4e | b. Online shopping
c. A Stake in the Outcome | d. Electronic commerce

6. _________ of the learning curve effect and the closely related experience curve effect express the relationship between equations for experience and efficiency or between efficiency gains and investment in the effort. The experience of 'learning curves' was first observed by the 19th Century German psychologist Hermann Ebbinghaus according to the difficulty of memorizing varying numbers of verbal stimuli, and subsequent learning about the complex processes of learning are discussed in the

.

The rule used for representing the learning curve effect states that the more times a task has been performed, the less time will be required on each subsequent iteration.

a. Point biserial correlation coefficient
b. Distribution
c. Spatial Decision Support Systems
d. Models

7. In economics, the term _________ refers to situations where the advancement of a qualified person within the hierarchy of an organization is stopped at a lower level because of some form of discrimination, most commonly sexism or racism, but since the term was coined, '_________' has also come to describe the limited advancement of the deaf, blind, disabled, aged and sexual minorities.It is an unofficial, invisible barrier that prevents women and minorities from advancing in businesses.

This situation is referred to as a 'ceiling' as there is a limitation blocking upward advancement, and 'glass' (transparent) because the limitation is not immediately apparent and is normally an unwritten and unofficial policy. This invisible barrier continues to exist, even though there are no explicit obstacles keeping minorities from acquiring advanced job positions - there are no advertisements that specifically say 'no minorities hired at this establishment', nor are there any formal orders that say 'minorities are not qualified' - but they do lie beneath the surface.

a. 1990 Clean Air Act
b. Glass Ceiling
c. 33 Strategies of War
d. 28-hour day

8. The U.S. _________ is an independent agency of the United States government which holds primary responsibility for enforcing the federal securities laws and regulating the securities industry, the nation's stock and options exchanges, and other electronic securities markets. The SEC was created by section 4 of the Securities Exchange Act of 1934 (now codified as 15 U.S.C. Â§ 78d and commonly referred to as the 1934 Act.)

a. Securities and Exchange Commission
b. 28-hour day
c. 1990 Clean Air Act
d. 33 Strategies of War

9. _________ was a writer, management consultant, and self-described 'social ecologist.' Widely considered to be 'the father of modern management,' his 39 books and countless scholarly and popular articles explored how humans are organized across all sectors of society--in business, government and the nonprofit world. His writings have predicted many of the major developments of the late twentieth century, including privatization and decentralization; the rise of Japan to economic world power; the decisive importance of marketing; and the emergence of the information society with its necessity of lifelong learning. In 1959, Drucker coined the term 'knowledge worker' and later in his life considered knowledge work productivity to be the next frontier of management.

a. Jacques Al-Salawat Nasruddin Nasser
b. Chrissie Hynde
c. Debora L. Spar
d. Peter Ferdinand Drucker

10. _________ is an American writer on business management practices, best-known for, In Search of Excellence (co-authored with Robert H. Waterman, Jr.)

Peters was born in Baltimore, Maryland. He went to Severn School for High School and attended Cornell University, receiving a bachelor's degree in civil engineering in 1965, and a master's degree in 1966.

a. Abraham Harold Maslow
b. Adam Smith
c. Affiliation
d. Thomas J. Peters

11. A chief executive officer (_________) or chief executive is one of the highest-ranking corporate officer (executive) or administrator in charge of total management. An individual selected as President and _________ of a corporation, company, organization, or agency, reports to the board of directors. In internal communication and press releases, many companies capitalize the term and those of other high positions, even when they are not proper nouns.

a. Chief executive officer
b. Portfolio manager
c. Director of communications
d. CEO

12. In decision theory and estimation theory, the _________ of an estimator, $\hat{\theta}$, of an unknown parameter of the distribution, θ, is the expected value of the loss function

$$R(\theta,\hat{\theta}) = \mathbb{E}_\theta L(\theta,\hat{\theta}) = \int L(\theta,\hat{\theta})\, dP_\theta.$$

where dP_θ is a probability measure parametrized by θ.

- For a scalar parameter θ and a quadratic loss function,

$$L(\theta,\hat{\theta}) = (\theta - \hat{\theta})^2$$

the _________ function becomes the mean squared error of the estimate,

$$R(\theta,\hat{\theta}) = E_\theta(\theta - \hat{\theta})^2$$

- In density estimation, the unknown parameter is probability density itself. The loss function is typically chosen to be a norm in an appropriate function space. For example, for L^2 norm,

$$L(f,\hat{f}) = \|f - \hat{f}\|_2^2$$

the _________ function becomes the mean integrated squared error

$$R(f,\hat{f}) = E\|f - \hat{f}\|^2$$

.

a. Risk
b. Risk aversion
c. Financial modeling
d. Linear model

13. _________ is the largest book retailer in the United States, operating mainly through its Barnes ' Noble Booksellers chain of bookstores headquartered in lower Fifth Avenue in Manhattan.

The company operates the chain of small 'B.

a. 1990 Clean Air Act
b. 33 Strategies of War
c. 28-hour day
d. Barnes ' Noble, Inc.

14. A _________ is a decision support tool that uses a tree-like graph or model of decisions and their possible consequences, including chance event outcomes, resource costs, and utility. _________s are commonly used in operations research, specifically in decision analysis, to help identify a strategy most likely to reach a goal. Another use of _________s is as a descriptive means for calculating conditional probabilities.

a. 1990 Clean Air Act
b. 33 Strategies of War
c. 28-hour day
d. Decision tree

15. Appraisal is the third and last stage in using formal decision methods. The objective of the appraisal stage is for the decision maker to develop insight into the decision and determine a clear course of action. Much of the insight developed in this stage results from exploring the implications of the formal _________ developed during the formulation stage (i.e., from mining the model.)

a. Kepner-Tregoe
b. Decision Matrix
c. Nominal group technique
d. Decision model

16. While the full name of the Swiss verein is Deloitte Touche Tohmatsu, in 1989 it initially branded itself _________ and then simply Deloitte. In 2003 the rebranding campaign was commissioned by Bill Parrett, the then CEO of DTT, and led by Jerry Leamon, the global Clients and Markets leader.

Deloitte member firms offer services in the following functions, with country-specific variations on their legal implementation (i.e. all operating within a single company or through separate legal entities operating as subsidiaries of an umbrella legal entity for the country.)

a. 1990 Clean Air Act
b. Deloitte ' Touche
c. 33 Strategies of War
d. 28-hour day

17. _________ is a form of communication that typically attempts to persuade potential customers to purchase or to consume more of a particular brand of product or service. 'While now central to the contemporary global economy and the reproduction of global production networks, it is only quite recently that _________ has been more than a marginal influence on patterns of sales and production. The formation of modern _________ was intimately bound up with the emergence of new forms of monopoly capitalism around the end of the 19th and beginning of the 20th century as one element in corporate strategies to create, organize and where possible control markets, especially for mass produced consumer goods.

a. Advertising
b. A Stake in the Outcome
c. A4e
d. AAAI

18. _________ is a group creativity technique designed to generate a large number of ideas for the solution of a problem. The method was first popularized in the late 1930s by Alex Faickney Osborn in a book called Applied Imagination. Osborn proposed that groups could double their creative output with _________.

a. Abraham Harold Maslow
b. Adam Smith
c. Brainstorming
d. Affiliation

19. _________ is decision making in groups consisting of multiple members/entities. The challenge of group decision is deciding what action a group should take. There are various systems designed to solve this problem.

a. Control of Substances Hazardous to Health Regulations 2002
b. Collaborative Planning, Forecasting and Replenishment
c. Genbutsu
d. Groups decision making

20. The _________ is a decision making method for use among groups of many sizes, who want to make their decision quickly, as by a vote, but want everyone's opinions taken into account (as opposed to traditional voting, where only the largest group is considered) . The method of tallying is the difference. First, every member of the group gives their view of the solution, with a short explanation.

a. Belief decision matrix
b. Hierarchical Decision Process
c. Decision model
d. Nominal group technique

21. The _________ is a systematic, interactive forecasting method which relies on a panel of independent experts. The carefully selected experts answer questionnaires in two or more rounds. After each round, a facilitator provides an anonymous summary of the experts' forecasts from the previous round as well as the reasons they provided for their judgments.

a. Hoshin Kanri
b. Learning organization
c. Quality function deployment
d. Delphi method

22. The 'business case for _________', theorizes that in a global marketplace, a company that employs a diverse workforce (both men and women, people of many generations, people from ethnically and racially diverse backgrounds etc.) is better able to understand the demographics of the marketplace it serves and is thus better equipped to thrive in that marketplace than a company that has a more limited range of employee demographics.

An additional corollary suggests that a company that supports the _________ of its workforce can also improve employee satisfaction, productivity and retention.

a. Kanban
b. Trademark
c. Virtual team
d. Diversity

23. _________ is a business management strategy aimed at embedding awareness of quality in all organizational processes. _________ has been widely used in manufacturing, education, hospitals, call centers, government, and service industries, as well as NASA space and science programs.

As defined by the International Organization for Standardization (ISO):

> '_________ is a management approach for an organization, centered on quality, based on the participation of all its members and aiming at long-term success through customer satisfaction, and benefits to all members of the organization and to society.' ISO 8402:1994

One major aim is to reduce variation from every process so that greater consistency of effort is obtained. (Royse, D., Thyer, B., Padgett D., ' Logan T., 2006)

a. Quality management
b. 28-hour day
c. 1990 Clean Air Act
d. Total quality management

24. The U.S. _________ is a federal agency whose goal is ending employment discrimination. The _________ investigates discrimination complaints based on an individual's race, color, national origin, religion, sex, age, disability and retaliation for reporting and/or opposing a discriminatory practice. The Commission is also tasked with filing suits on behalf of alleged victim(s) of discrimination against employers and as an adjudicatory for claims of discrimination brought against federal agencies.

a. ARCO
b. Airbus SAS
c. Airbus Industrie
d. Equal Employment Opportunity Commission

25. Procter is a surname, and may also refer to:

- Bryan Waller Procter (pseud. Barry Cornwall), English poet
- Goodwin Procter, American law firm
- _________, consumer products multinational

.

a. Downstream
b. Master and Servant Acts
c. Strict liability
d. Procter ' Gamble

26. _________ is an inventory strategy that strives to improve the return on investment of a business by reducing in-process inventory and its associated carrying costs. To meet _________ objectives, the process relies on signals between different points in the process. This means the process is often driven by a series of signals, or Kanban , which tell production when to make the next part. Kanban are usually 'tickets' but can be simple visual signals, such as the presence or absence of a part on a shelf. Implemented correctly, _________ can dramatically improve a manufacturing organization's return on investment, quality, and efficiency.

a. 28-hour day
b. 1990 Clean Air Act
c. Just-in-time
d. 33 Strategies of War

1. An _________ is a mostly hierarchical concept of subordination of entities that collaborate and contribute to serve one common aim.

Organizations are a variant of clustered entities. The structure of an organization is usually set up in many a styles, dependent on their objectives and ambience.

a. Open shop
b. Organizational development
c. Informal organization
d. Organizational structure

2. _________ is an advertisement in which a particular product specifically mentions a competitor by name for the express purpose of showing why the competitor is inferior to the product naming it.

This should not be confused with parody advertisements, where a fictional product is being advertised for the purpose of poking fun at the particular advertisement, nor should it be confused with the use of a coined brand name for the purpose of comparing the product without actually naming an actual competitor. ('Wikipedia tastes better and is less filling than the Encyclopedia Galactica.')

In the 1980s, during what has been referred to as the cola wars, soft-drink manufacturer Pepsi ran a series of advertisements where people, caught on hidden camera, in a blind taste test, chose Pepsi over rival Coca-Cola.

a. 33 Strategies of War
b. 1990 Clean Air Act
c. Comparative advertising
d. 28-hour day

3. _________ is a fixed set of rules of intra-organization procedures and structures. As such, it is usually set out in writing, with a language of rules that ostensibly leave little discretion for interpretation. In some societies and in some organization, such rules may be strictly followed; in others, they may be little more than an empty formalism.

a. 1990 Clean Air Act
b. 33 Strategies of War
c. 28-hour day
d. Formal organization

4. _________ can be regarded as an outcome of mental processes (cognitive process) leading to the selection of a course of action among several alternatives. Every _________ process produces a final choice. The output can be an action or an opinion of choice.

a. 33 Strategies of War
b. Decision making
c. 28-hour day
d. 1990 Clean Air Act

5. _________ is the corporate management term for the act of reorganizing the legal, ownership, operational, or other structures of a company for the purpose of making it more profitable, or better organized for its present needs. Alternate reasons for _________ include a change of ownership or ownership structure, demerger repositioning debt _________ and financial _________.

a. Restructuring
b. Net worth
c. Market value added
d. Market value

6. _________ is subcontracting a process, such as product design or manufacturing, to a third-party company. The decision to outsource is often made in the interest of lowering cost or making better use of time and energy costs, redirecting or conserving energy directed at the competencies of a particular business, or to make more efficient use of land, labor, capital, (information) technology and resources. _________ became part of the business lexicon during the 1980s.

a. Opinion leadership
b. Outsourcing
c. Operant conditioning
d. Unemployment insurance

7. A chief executive officer (_________) or chief executive is one of the highest-ranking corporate officer (executive) or administrator in charge of total management. An individual selected as President and _________ of a corporation, company, organization, or agency, reports to the board of directors. In internal communication and press releases, many companies capitalize the term and those of other high positions, even when they are not proper nouns.

a. CEO
b. Chief executive officer
c. Portfolio manager
d. Director of communications

8. In a military context, the _________ is the line of authority and responsibility along which orders are passed within a military unit and between different units. The term is also used in a civilian management context describing comparable hierarchical structures of authority.

a. 1990 Clean Air Act
b. Chain of command
c. 28-hour day
d. French leave

9. _________ is an organization's process of defining its strategy and making decisions on allocating its resources to pursue this strategy, including its capital and people. Various business analysis techniques can be used in _________, including SWOT analysis (Strengths, Weaknesses, Opportunities, and Threats) and PEST analysis (Political, Economic, Social, and Technological analysis) or STEER analysis involving Socio-cultural, Technological, Economic, Ecological, and Regulatory factors and EPISTEL (Environment, Political, Informatic, Social, Technological, Economic and Legal)

_________ is the formal consideration of an organization's future course. All _________ deals with at least one of three key questions:

1. 'What do we do?'
2. 'For whom do we do it?'
3. 'How do we excel?'

In business _________, the third question is better phrased 'How can we beat or avoid competition?'. (Bradford and Duncan, page 1.)

a. Strategic planning
b. 28-hour day
c. 1990 Clean Air Act
d. 33 Strategies of War

10. A _________ or business method is a collection of related, structured activities or tasks that produce a specific service or product (serve a particular goal) for a particular customer or customers. It often can be visualized with a flowchart as a sequence of activities.

There are three types of _________es:

1. Management processes, the processes that govern the operation of a system. Typical management processes include 'Corporate Governance' and 'Strategic Management'.
2. Operational processes, processes that constitute the core business and create the primary value stream. Typical operational processes are Purchasing, Manufacturing, Marketing, and Sales.
3. Supporting processes, which support the core processes. Examples include Accounting, Recruitment, Technical support.

A _________ begins with a customer's need and ends with a customer's need fulfillment. Process oriented organizations break down the barriers of structural departments and try to avoid functional silos.

a. Business process
b. 33 Strategies of War
c. 1990 Clean Air Act
d. 28-hour day

11. _________ refers to the process of grouping activities into departments.

Division of labour creates specialists who need coordination. This coordination is facilitated by grouping specialists together in departments.

a. Maximum wage
b. Decent work
c. Division of labour
d. Departmentalization

12. A _________ is a relatively new executive level position at a corporation, company, organization typically reporting directly to the CEO or board of directors. The _________ is responsible for a brand's image, experience, and promise, and propagating it throughout all aspects of the company. The brand officer oversees marketing, advertising, design, public relations and customer service departments.

a. Purchasing manager
b. Director of communications
c. Chief executive officer
d. Chief brand officer

13. An _________, or organogram(me)) is a diagram that shows the structure of an organization and the relationships and relative ranks of its parts and positions/jobs. The term is also used for similar diagrams, for example ones showing the different elements of a field of knowledge or a group of languages. The French Encyclopédie had one of the first _________s of knowledge in general.

a. A4e
b. A Stake in the Outcome
c. AAAI
d. Organizational chart

14. The _________ is a standardized, on-scene, all-hazard incident management concept. It is a management protocol originally designed for emergency management agencies in the United States which was later federalized there. It has since been adopted by agencies in other countries.

a. A4e
b. A Stake in the Outcome
c. AAAI
d. Incident Command Structure

15. _________ or lean production, which is often known simply as 'Lean', is a production practice that considers the expenditure of resources for any goal other than the creation of value for the end customer to be wasteful, and thus a target for elimination. Working from the perspective of the customer who consumes a product or service, 'value' is defined as any action or process that a customer would be willing to pay for. Basically, lean is centered around creating more value with less work.

a. Six Sigma
b. Production line
c. Theory of constraints
d. Lean Manufacturing

16. _________ is individual power based on a high level of identification with, admiration of, or respect for the powerholder.

Nationalism, Patriotism, Celebrities and well-respected people are examples of _________ in effect.

_________ is one of the Five Bases of Social Power, as defined by Bertram Raven and his colleagues[1] in 1959.

a. 33 Strategies of War
b. 28-hour day
c. 1990 Clean Air Act
d. Referent power

17. _________ is a form of communication that typically attempts to persuade potential customers to purchase or to consume more of a particular brand of product or service. 'While now central to the contemporary global economy and the reproduction of global production networks, it is only quite recently that _________ has been more than a marginal influence on patterns of sales and production. The formation of modern _________ was intimately bound up with the emergence of new forms of monopoly capitalism around the end of the 19th and beginning of the 20th century as one element in corporate strategies to create, organize and where possible control markets, especially for mass produced consumer goods.

a. A4e
b. AAAI
c. A Stake in the Outcome
d. Advertising

18. _________ is one of the managerial functions like planning, organizing, staffing and directing. It is an important function because it helps to check the errors and to take the corrective action so that deviation from standards are minimized and stated goals of the organization are achieved in desired manner.According to modern concepts, _________ is a foreseeing action whereas earlier concept of _________ was used only when errors were detected. _________ in management means setting standards, measuring actual performance and taking corrective action.

a. Turnover
b. Schedule of reinforcement
c. Decision tree pruning
d. Control

19. _________ is a term originating in military organization theory, but now used more commonly in business management, particularly human resource management. _________ refers to the number of subordinates a supervisor has.

In the hierarchical business organization of the past it was not uncommon to see average spans of 1 to 10 or even less. That is, one manager supervised ten employees on average.

a. Mentoring
b. Senior management
c. CIFMS
d. Span of control

20. _________ is the process by which the activities of an organisation, particularly those regarding decision-making, become concentrated within a particular location and/or group.

a. Chief operating officer
b. Centralization
c. Corner office
d. Product innovation

21. _________ consists of the mental process of thinking involved with the process of judging the merits of multiple options and selecting one of them for action. Some simple examples include deciding whether to get up in the morning or go back to sleep, or selecting a given route for a journey. More complex examples (often decisions that affect what a person thinks or their core beliefs) include choosing a lifestyle, religious affiliation, or political position.

a. Trade study
b. Championship mobilization
c. Groups decision making
d. Choice

22. _________ is the process of dispersing decision-making governance closer to the people or citizen. It includes the dispersal of administration or governance in sectors or areas like engineering, management science, political science, political economy, sociology and economics. _________ is also possible in the dispersal of population and employment.

a. Business plan
b. Frenemy
c. Formula for Change
d. Decentralization

23. The _________ was a period in the late 18th and early 19th centuries when major changes in agriculture, manufacturing, mining, and transportation had a profound effect on the socioeconomic and cultural conditions in Britain. The changes subsequently spread throughout Europe, North America, and eventually the world. The onset of the _________ marked a major turning point in human society; almost every aspect of daily life was eventually influenced in some way.

a. Industrial Revolution
b. Adam Smith
c. Abraham Harold Maslow
d. Affiliation

24. The _________ is the interlocking social structure that governs how people work together in practice. It is the aggregate of behaviors, interactions, norms, personal and professional connections through which work gets done and relationships are built among people who share a common organizational affiliation or cluster of affiliations. It consists of a dynamic set of personal relationships, social networks, communities of common interest, and emotional sources of motivation. The _________ evolves organically and spontaneously in response to changes in the work environment, the flux of people through its porous boundaries, and the complex social dynamics of its members.

a. Informal organization
b. Union shop
c. Open shop
d. Organizational effectiveness

25. The U.S. _________ is a federal agency whose goal is ending employment discrimination. The _________ investigates discrimination complaints based on an individual's race, color, national origin, religion, sex, age, disability and retaliation for reporting and/or opposing a discriminatory practice. The Commission is also tasked with filing suits on behalf of alleged victim(s) of discrimination against employers and as an adjudicatory for claims of discrimination brought against federal agencies.

a. Airbus Industrie
b. ARCO
c. Airbus SAS
d. Equal Employment Opportunity Commission

1. _________ is the temporary suspension or permanent termination of employment of an employee or (more commonly) a group of employees for business reasons, such as the decision that certain positions are no longer necessary or a business slow-down or interruption in work. Originally the term '_________' referred exclusively to a temporary interruption in work, as when factory work cyclically falls off. However, in recent times the term can also refer to the permanent elimination of a position.

a. Retirement
b. Termination of employment
c. Wrongful dismissal
d. Layoff

2. _________ is a method by which the job performance of an employee is evaluated _________ is a part of career development.

_________s are regular reviews of employee performance within organizations

Generally, the aims of a _________ are to:

- Give feedback on performance to employees.
- Identify employee training needs.
- Document criteria used to allocate organizational rewards.
- Form a basis for personnel decisions: salary increases, promotions, disciplinary actions, etc.
- Provide the opportunity for organizational diagnosis and development.
- Facilitate communication between employee and administraton
- Validate selection techniques and human resource policies to meet federal Equal Employment Opportunity requirements.

A common approach to assessing performance is to use a numerical or scalar rating system whereby managers are asked to score an individual against a number of objectives/attributes. In some companies, employees receive assessments from their manager, peers, subordinates and customers while also performing a self assessment.

a. Progressive discipline
b. Human resource management
c. Personnel management
d. Performance appraisal

3. _________ is a business management strategy, initially implemented by Motorola, that today enjoys widespread application in many sectors of industry.

_________ seeks to improve the quality of process outputs by identifying and removing the causes of defects (errors) and variation in manufacturing and business processes. It uses a set of quality management methods, including statistical methods, and creates a special infrastructure of people within the organization ('Black Belts' etc.)

a. Production line
b. Takt time
c. Theory of constraints
d. Six Sigma

4. The _________ of 1967, Pub. L. No. 90-202, 81 Stat. 602 (Dec. 15, 1967), codified as Chapter 14 of Title 29 of the United States Code, 29 U.S.C. Â§ 621 through 29 U.S.C. Â§ 634 (ADEA), prohibits employment discrimination against persons 40 years of age or older in the United States). The law also sets standards for pensions and benefits provided by employers and requires that information about the needs of older workers be provided to the general public.

a. Unemployment and Farm Relief Act
b. Extra time
c. Age Discrimination in Employment Act
d. Undue hardship

5. _________ is a contract between two parties, one being the employer and the other being the employee. An employee may be defined as: 'A person in the service of another under any contract of hire, express or implied, oral or written, where the employer has the power or right to control and direct the employee in the material details of how the work is to be performed.' Black's Law Dictionary page 471 (5th ed. 1979.)

a. Employment counsellor
b. Employment rate
c. Exit interview
d. Employment

6. A _________ is the term given to a company that facilitates the learning of its members and continuously transforms itself. _________s develop as a result of the pressures facing modern organizations and enables them to remain competitive in the business environment. A _________ has five main features; systems thinking, personal mastery, mental models, shared vision and team learning.

a. 1990 Clean Air Act
b. Learning organization
c. Quality function deployment
d. Hoshin Kanri

7. _________ is the life cycle of an organization from birth level to the termination.

There are five level/stages in any organization.

1. Birth
2. Growth
3. Maturity
4. Decline
5. Death

According to Richard L. Daft there are four stages in an _________.

The four stages are:

1. Entrepreneurial stage -> Crisis: Need for leadership
2. Collectivity stage -> Crisis: Need for delegation
3. Formalization stage -> Crisis: Too much red tape
4. Elaboration stage -> Crisis: Need for revitalization

(Richard L. Daft, Understanding the Theory and Design of Organizations, first edition 2007, ISBN 0-324-42271-7)

a. AAAI
b. A Stake in the Outcome
c. Organizational life cycle
d. A4e

8. _________ is the production of large amounts of standardized products, including and especially on assembly lines. The concepts of _________ are applied to various kinds of products, from fluids and particulates handled in bulk to discrete solid parts to assemblies of such parts

_________ of assemblies typically uses electric-motor-powered moving tracks or conveyor belts to move partially complete products to workers, who perform simple repetitive tasks.

a. 28-hour day
b. Mass production
c. 1990 Clean Air Act
d. 33 Strategies of War

9. An _________ is a mostly hierarchical concept of subordination of entities that collaborate and contribute to serve one common aim.

Organizations are a variant of clustered entities. The structure of an organization is usually set up in many a styles, dependent on their objectives and ambience.

a. Open shop
b. Organizational development
c. Informal organization
d. Organizational structure

10. A _________ system is a manufacturing system in which there is some amount of flexibility that allows the system to react in the case of changes, whether predicted or unpredicted. This flexibility is generally considered to fall into two categories, which both contain numerous subcategories.

The first category, machine flexibility, covers the system's ability to be changed to produce new product types, and ability to change the order of operations executed on a part. The second category is called routing flexibility, which consists of the ability to use multiple machines to perform the same operation on a part, as well as the system's ability to absorb large-scale changes, such as in volume, capacity, or capability.

a. Manufacturing resource planning
b. Homeworkers
c. Jidoka
d. Flexible manufacturing

11. In finance, an _________ is a contract between a buyer and a seller that gives the buyer the right--but not the obligation--to buy or to sell a particular asset (the underlying asset) at a later day at an agreed price. In return for granting the _________, the seller collects a payment (the premium) from the buyer. A call _________ gives the buyer the right to buy the underlying asset; a put _________ gives the buyer of the _________ the right to sell the underlying asset.

a. A4e
b. AAAI
c. A Stake in the Outcome
d. Option

12. _________ can be regarded as an outcome of mental processes (cognitive process) leading to the selection of a course of action among several alternatives. Every _________ process produces a final choice. The output can be an action or an opinion of choice.

a. 1990 Clean Air Act
b. 33 Strategies of War
c. 28-hour day
d. Decision making

13. _________ is decision making in groups consisting of multiple members/entities. The challenge of group decision is deciding what action a group should take. There are various systems designed to solve this problem.

a. Groups decision making
b. Control of Substances Hazardous to Health Regulations 2002
c. Collaborative Planning, Forecasting and Replenishment
d. Genbutsu

14. _________ is 'interfirm coordination that is characterized by organic or informal social systems, in contrast to bureaucratic structures within firms and formal contractual relationships between them.(Gerlach, 1992:64; Nohria, 1992)' A useful survey of network organization theory appears in Van Alstyne (1997).

The concepts of privatization, public private partnership, and contracting are defined in this context.

As a concept, _________ explains increased efficiency and reduced agency problems for organizations existing in highly turbulent environments . Due to the rapid pace of modern society and competitive pressures from globalization, _________ has gained prominence and development among sociological theorists. As a concept, _________ explains increased efficiency and reduced agency problems for organizations existing in highly turbulent environments.

a. 28-hour day
b. 33 Strategies of War
c. 1990 Clean Air Act
d. Network governance

15. Procter is a surname, and may also refer to:

- Bryan Waller Procter (pseud. Barry Cornwall), English poet
- Goodwin Procter, American law firm
- _________, consumer products multinational

.

a. Master and Servant Acts
b. Downstream
c. Procter ' Gamble
d. Strict liability

16. _________ is an idea in the field of Organizational studies and management which describes the psychology, attitudes, experiences, beliefs and Values (personal and cultural values) of an organization. It has been defined as 'the specific collection of values and norms that are shared by people and groups in an organization and that control the way they interact with each other and with stakeholders outside the organization.'

This definition continues to explain organizational values also known as 'beliefs and ideas about what kinds of goals members of an organization should pursue and ideas about the appropriate kinds or standards of behavior organizational members should use to achieve these goals. From organizational values develop organizational norms, guidelines or expectations that prescribe appropriate kinds of behavior by employees in particular situations and control the behavior of organizational members towards one another.'

_________ is not the same as corporate culture.

a. Organizational culture
b. Organizational effectiveness
c. Organizational development
d. Union shop

17. _________ is an American writer on business management practices, best-known for, In Search of Excellence (co-authored with Robert H. Waterman, Jr.)

Peters was born in Baltimore, Maryland. He went to Severn School for High School and attended Cornell University, receiving a bachelor's degree in civil engineering in 1965, and a master's degree in 1966.

a. Adam Smith
b. Abraham Harold Maslow
c. Affiliation
d. Thomas J. Peters

18. A _________ is an alliance among individuals or groups, during which they cooperate in joint action, each in his own self-interest, joining forces together for a common cause. This alliance may be temporary or a matter of convenience. A _________ thus differs from a more formal covenant.

a. 1990 Clean Air Act
b. 28-hour day
c. 33 Strategies of War
d. Coalition

19. While the full name of the Swiss verein is Deloitte Touche Tohmatsu, in 1989 it initially branded itself _________ and then simply Deloitte. In 2003 the rebranding campaign was commissioned by Bill Parrett, the then CEO of DTT, and led by Jerry Leamon, the global Clients and Markets leader.

Deloitte member firms offer services in the following functions, with country-specific variations on their legal implementation (i.e. all operating within a single company or through separate legal entities operating as subsidiaries of an umbrella legal entity for the country.)

a. 1990 Clean Air Act
b. 28-hour day
c. 33 Strategies of War
d. Deloitte ' Touche

20. A chief executive officer (_________) or chief executive is one of the highest-ranking corporate officer (executive) or administrator in charge of total management. An individual selected as President and _________ of a corporation, company, organization, or agency, reports to the board of directors. In internal communication and press releases, many companies capitalize the term and those of other high positions, even when they are not proper nouns.

a. Director of communications
b. Portfolio manager
c. Chief executive officer
d. CEO

21. _________ is a broad label that refers to any individuals or households that use goods and services generated within the economy. The concept of a _________ is used in different contexts, so that the usage and significance of the term may vary.

Typically when business people and economists talk of _________s they are talking about person as _________, an aggregated commodity item with little individuality other than that expressed in the buy/not-buy decision.

a. Consumer
b. 28-hour day
c. 33 Strategies of War
d. 1990 Clean Air Act

22. The _________ of 1938 (_________, ch. 676, 52 Stat. 1060, June 25, 1938, 29 U.S.C. ch.8), also called the Wages and Hours Bill, is United States federal law that applies to employees engaged in interstate commerce or employed by an enterprise engaged in commerce or in the production of goods for commerce, unless the employer can claim an exemption from coverage. The _________ established a national minimum wage, guaranteed time and a half for overtime in certain jobs, and prohibited most employment of minors in 'oppressive child labor,' a term defined in the statute.

a. Family and Medical Leave Act of 1993
b. Fair Labor Standards Act
c. Joint venture
d. Board of directors

23. _________ are conventions, treaties and recommendations designed to eliminate unjust and inhumane labour practices. The primary inernational agency charged with developing such standards is the International Labour Organization (ILO.) Established in 1919, the ILO advocates international standards as essential for the eradication of labour conditions involving 'injustice, hardship and privation'.

a. International labour standards
b. Anaconda Copper
c. Airbus Industrie
d. Airbus SAS

24. The U.S. _________ is a federal agency whose goal is ending employment discrimination. The _________ investigates discrimination complaints based on an individual's race, color, national origin, religion, sex, age, disability and retaliation for reporting and/or opposing a discriminatory practice. The Commission is also tasked with filing suits on behalf of alleged victim(s) of discrimination against employers and as an adjudicatory for claims of discrimination brought against federal agencies.

a. Airbus Industrie
b. ARCO
c. Airbus SAS
d. Equal Employment Opportunity Commission

25. In sociology, anthropology and cultural studies, a _________ is a group of people with a culture (whether distinct or hidden) which differentiates them from the larger culture to which they belong. If a particular _________ is characterized by a systematic opposition to the dominant culture, it may be described as a counterculture.

As early as 1950, David Riesman distinguished between a majority, 'which passively accepted commercially provided styles and meanings, and a '_________' which actively sought a minority style ...

a. 33 Strategies of War
b. Subculture
c. 1990 Clean Air Act
d. 28-hour day

26. A _________ or business method is a collection of related, structured activities or tasks that produce a specific service or product (serve a particular goal) for a particular customer or customers. It often can be visualized with a flowchart as a sequence of activities.

There are three types of _________es:

1. Management processes, the processes that govern the operation of a system. Typical management processes include 'Corporate Governance' and 'Strategic Management'.
2. Operational processes, processes that constitute the core business and create the primary value stream. Typical operational processes are Purchasing, Manufacturing, Marketing, and Sales.
3. Supporting processes, which support the core processes. Examples include Accounting, Recruitment, Technical support.

A _________ begins with a customer's need and ends with a customer's need fulfillment. Process oriented organizations break down the barriers of structural departments and try to avoid functional silos.

a. 33 Strategies of War
b. 1990 Clean Air Act
c. 28-hour day
d. Business process

27. _________ is, in computer science and management, an approach aiming at improvements by means of elevating efficiency and effectiveness of the business process that exist within and across organizations. The key to _________ is for organizations to look at their business processes from a 'clean slate' perspective and determine how they can best construct these processes to improve how they conduct business. _________ Cycle.

_________ is also known as _________, Business Process Redesign, Business Transformation, or Business Process Change Management.

a. Personal management interview
b. Horizontal integration
c. Product life cycle
d. Business process reengineering

28. _________ is a recursive process where two or more people or organizations work together in an intersection of common goals -- for example, an intellectual endeavor that is creative in nature--by sharing knowledge, learning and building consensus. _________ does not require leadership and can sometimes bring better results through decentralization and egalitarianism. In particular, teams that work collaboratively can obtain greater resources, recognition and reward when facing competition for finite resources._________ is also present in opposing goals exhibiting the notion of adversarial _________, though this is not a common case for using the term.

a. 28-hour day
b. 1990 Clean Air Act
c. Collaboration
d. Collectivism

29. _________ is a layer of management in an organization whose primary job responsibility is to monitor activities of subordinates while reporting to upper management.

In pre-computer times, _________ would collect information from junior management and reassemble it for senior management. With the advent of inexpensive PCs this function has been taken over by e-business systems.

a. Theory Y
b. Community management
c. Continuous monitoring
d. Middle management

30. _________ is a form of communication that typically attempts to persuade potential customers to purchase or to consume more of a particular brand of product or service. 'While now central to the contemporary global economy and the reproduction of global production networks, it is only quite recently that _________ has been more than a marginal influence on patterns of sales and production. The formation of modern _________ was intimately bound up with the emergence of new forms of monopoly capitalism around the end of the 19th and beginning of the 20th century as one element in corporate strategies to create, organize and where possible control markets, especially for mass produced consumer goods.

a. A Stake in the Outcome
b. A4e
c. Advertising
d. AAAI

31. In economics, the term _________ refers to situations where the advancement of a qualified person within the hierarchy of an organization is stopped at a lower level because of some form of discrimination, most commonly sexism or racism, but since the term was coined, '_________' has also come to describe the limited advancement of the deaf, blind, disabled, aged and sexual minorities.It is an unofficial, invisible barrier that prevents women and minorities from advancing in businesses.

This situation is referred to as a 'ceiling' as there is a limitation blocking upward advancement, and 'glass' (transparent) because the limitation is not immediately apparent and is normally an unwritten and unofficial policy. This invisible barrier continues to exist, even though there are no explicit obstacles keeping minorities from acquiring advanced job positions - there are no advertisements that specifically say 'no minorities hired at this establishment', nor are there any formal orders that say 'minorities are not qualified' - but they do lie beneath the surface.

a. 1990 Clean Air Act
b. Glass Ceiling
c. 33 Strategies of War
d. 28-hour day

32. _________ is an organization's process of defining its strategy and making decisions on allocating its resources to pursue this strategy, including its capital and people. Various business analysis techniques can be used in _________, including SWOT analysis (Strengths, Weaknesses, Opportunities, and Threats) and PEST analysis (Political, Economic, Social, and Technological analysis) or STEER analysis involving Socio-cultural, Technological, Economic, Ecological, and Regulatory factors and EPISTEL (Environment, Political, Informatic, Social, Technological, Economic and Legal)

_________ is the formal consideration of an organization's future course. All _________ deals with at least one of three key questions:

1. 'What do we do?'
2. 'For whom do we do it?'
3. 'How do we excel?'

In business _________, the third question is better phrased 'How can we beat or avoid competition?'. (Bradford and Duncan, page 1.)

a. 28-hour day
b. 1990 Clean Air Act
c. 33 Strategies of War
d. Strategic planning

33. _________ is an area of knowledge within organizational theory that studies models and theories about the way an organization learns and adapts.

In Organizational development (OD), learning is a characteristic of an adaptive organization, i.e., an organization that is able to sense changes in signals from its environment (both internal and external) and adapt accordingly.

a. AAAI
b. Organizational learning
c. A4e
d. A Stake in the Outcome

34. _________ has been described as the 'process of social influence in which one person can enlist the aid and support of others in the accomplishment of a common task' . A definition more inclusive of followers comes from Alan Keith of Genentech who said '_________ is ultimately about creating a way for people to contribute to making something extraordinary happen.'

_________ is one of the most salient aspects of the organizational context. However, defining _________ has been challenging.

a. 1990 Clean Air Act
b. Situational leadership
c. 28-hour day
d. Leadership

35. The U.S. _________ is an independent agency of the United States government which holds primary responsibility for enforcing the federal securities laws and regulating the securities industry, the nation's stock and options exchanges, and other electronic securities markets. The SEC was created by section 4 of the Securities Exchange Act of 1934 (now codified as 15 U.S.C. Â§ 78d and commonly referred to as the 1934 Act.)

a. Securities and Exchange Commission
b. 1990 Clean Air Act
c. 33 Strategies of War
d. 28-hour day

36. As defined by Richard Beckhard, _________ is a planned, top-down, organization-wide effort to increase the organization's effectiveness and health. _________ is achieved through interventions in the organization's 'processes,' using behavioural science knowledge. According to Warren Bennis, _________ is a complex strategy intended to change the beliefs, attitudes, values, and structure of organizations so that they can better adapt to new technologies, markets, and challenges.

a. Organizational culture
b. Informal organization
c. Organizational structure
d. Organizational development

1. _________ is an integrated communications-based process through which individuals and communities discover that existing and newly-identified needs and wants may be satisfied by the products and services of others.

_________ is defined by the American _________ Association as the activity, set of institutions, and processes for creating, communicating, delivering, and exchanging offerings that have value for customers, clients, partners, and society at large. The term developed from the original meaning which referred literally to going to market, as in shopping, or going to a market to buy or sell goods or services.

a. Marketing
b. Disruptive technology
c. Customer relationship management
d. Market development

2. The term _________ collectively refers to all resources that determine the value and the competitiveness of an enterprise. As such, it includes as subsets the attributes that concur to building all financial statements as well as the balance sheet.

a. A Stake in the Outcome
b. Intellectual capital
c. A4e
d. AAAI

3. _________ is a contract between two parties, one being the employer and the other being the employee. An employee may be defined as: 'A person in the service of another under any contract of hire, express or implied, oral or written, where the employer has the power or right to control and direct the employee in the material details of how the work is to be performed.' Black's Law Dictionary page 471 (5th ed. 1979.)

a. Exit interview
b. Employment rate
c. Employment counsellor
d. Employment

4. _________ is the strategic and coherent approach to the management of an organisation's most valued assets - the people working there who individually and collectively contribute to the achievement of the objectives of the business. The terms '_________' and 'human resources' (HR) have largely replaced the term 'personnel management' as a description of the processes involved in managing people in organizations. In simple sense, _________ means employing people, developing their resources, utilizing, maintaining and compensating their services in tune with the job and organizational requirement.

a. Revolving door syndrome
b. Job knowledge
c. Human resource management
d. Progressive discipline

5. The term _________ was created by President Lyndon B. Johnson when he signed Executive Order 11246 on September 24, 1965, created to prohibit federal contractors from discriminating against employees on the basis of race, sex, creed, religion, color, or national origin. In more recent times, most employers have also added sexual orientation to the list of non-discrimination.

The Executive Order also required contractors to implement affirmative action plans to increase the participation of minorities and women in the workplace.

a. AAAI
b. A4e
c. A Stake in the Outcome
d. Equal Employment Opportunity

6. The U.S. _________ is a federal agency whose goal is ending employment discrimination. The _________ investigates discrimination complaints based on an individual's race, color, national origin, religion, sex, age, disability and retaliation for reporting and/or opposing a discriminatory practice. The Commission is also tasked with filing suits on behalf of alleged victim(s) of discrimination against employers and as an adjudicatory for claims of discrimination brought against federal agencies.

a. Airbus Industrie
b. Airbus SAS
c. ARCO
d. Equal Employment Opportunity Commission

7. _________ or lean production, which is often known simply as 'Lean', is a production practice that considers the expenditure of resources for any goal other than the creation of value for the end customer to be wasteful, and thus a target for elimination. Working from the perspective of the customer who consumes a product or service, 'value' is defined as any action or process that a customer would be willing to pay for. Basically, lean is centered around creating more value with less work.

a. Six Sigma
b. Production line
c. Theory of constraints
d. Lean Manufacturing

8. The _________ of 1990 (ADA) is the short title of United States (Pub.L. 101-336, 104 Stat. 327, enacted July 26, 1990), codified at 42 U.S.C. Â§ 12101 et seq. It was signed into law on July 26, 1990, by President George H. W. Bush, and later amended with changes effective January 1, 2009. The ADA is a wide-ranging civil rights law that prohibits, under certain circumstances, discrimination based on disability. It affords similar protections against discrimination to Americans with disabilities as the Civil Rights Act of 1964,

a. Equal Pay Act of 1963
b. Employment discrimination
c. Australian labour law
d. Americans with Disabilities Act

9. The _________ 1970 is an Act of the United Kingdom Parliament which prohibits any less favourable treatment between men and women in terms of pay and conditions of employment. It came into force on 29 December 1975. The term pay is interpreted in a broad sense to include, on top of wages, things like holidays, pension rights, company perks and some kinds of bonuses.

a. Architectural Barriers Act of 1968
b. Equal Pay Act
c. Oncale v. Sundowner Offshore Services
d. Australian labour law

10. _________ occurs when expectant women are fired, not hired, or otherwise discriminated against due to their pregnancy or intention to become pregnant. Common forms of _________ include not being hired due to visible pregnancy or likelihood of becoming pregnant, being fired after informing an employer of one's pregnancy, being fired after maternity leave, and receiving a pay dock due to pregnancy. In the United States, since 1978, employers are legally bound to provide what insurance, leave pay, and additional support that would be bestowed upon any employee with medical leave or disability.

a. Pregnancy Discrimination
b. 1990 Clean Air Act
c. 33 Strategies of War
d. 28-hour day

11. The U.S. _________ of 1973 prohibits discrimination on the basis of disability in programs conducted by Federal agencies, in programs receiving Federal financial assistance, in Federal employment, and in the employment practices of Federal contractors. The standards for determining employment discrimination under the _________ are the same as those used in title I of the Americans with Disabilities Act.

There are four key sections of the Act.

a. Rehabilitation Act
b. 28-hour day
c. 1990 Clean Air Act
d. 33 Strategies of War

12. _________ is the point where a person stops employment completely. A person may also semi-retire and keep some sort of _________ job, out of choice rather than necessity. This usually happens upon reaching a determined age, when physical conditions don't allow the person to work any more (by illness or accident), or even for personal choice (usually in the presence of an adequate pension or personal savings.)

a. Severance package
b. Termination of employment
c. Wrongful dismissal
d. Retirement

13. _________ is unwelcome harassment of a sexual nature, or based upon the receiving party's sex or gender. In some contexts or circumstances, _________ may be illegal. It includes a range of behavior from seemingly mild transgressions and annoyances to actual sexual abuse or sexual assault.

a. Hypernorms
b. 1990 Clean Air Act
c. 28-hour day
d. Sexual harassment

14. In employment law, a (BFOQ) (US) or bona fide occupational requirement (BFOR) (Canada) is a quality or an attribute that employers are allowed to consider when making decisions on the hiring and retention of employees - qualities that, when considered, in other contexts would be considered discriminatory and thus violating civil rights employment law.

In employment discrimination law in the United States, United States Code Title 29 , Chapter 14 (age discrimination in employment), section 623 (prohibition of age discrimination) establishes that 'It shall not be unlawful for an employer, employment agency, or labor organization (1) to take any action otherwise prohibited under subsections (a), (b), (c), or (e) of this section where age is a _________ reasonably necessary to the normal operation of the particular business, or where the differentiation is based on reasonable factors other than age, or where such practices involve an employee in a workplace in a foreign country, and compliance with such subsections would cause such employer, or a corporation controlled by such employer, to violate the laws of the country in which such workplace is located.'

One example of _________s are mandatory retirement ages for bus drivers and airline pilots, for safety reasons. Further, in advertising, a manufacturer of men's clothing may lawfully advertise for male models.

a. Bona fide occupational qualification
b. MacPherson v. Buick Motor Co.
c. Corporate governance
d. Sick leave

15. _________ is the concept of a person or group of people being in charge or in command of another person or group. This control is often granted to the senior person(s) due to experience or length of service in a given position, but it is not uncommon for a senior person(s) to have less experience or length of service than their subordinates.

More generally, '_________' can be a description of an individual's experience or length of service, and can thus be used to differentiate between individuals of otherwise equivalent status without placing them in a hierarchy of direct authority.

a. 1990 Clean Air Act
b. 33 Strategies of War
c. 28-hour day
d. Seniority

16.

The terms _________ and positive action refer to policies that take race, ethnicity, or gender into consideration in an attempt to promote equal opportunity. The focus of such policies ranges from employment and education to public contracting and health programs. The impetus towards _________ is twofold: to maximize diversity in all levels of society, along with its presumed benefits, and to redress perceived disadvantages due to overt, institutional, or involuntary discrimination.

a. Abraham Harold Maslow
b. Adam Smith
c. Affiliation
d. Affirmative action

17. In US employment law, _________ is defined as a substantially different rate of selection in hiring, promotion sex statistical significance tests, and/or practical significance tests. _________ is often used interchangeably with 'disparate impact,' which was a legal term coined in one of the most significant U.S. Supreme Court rulings on disparate or _________: Griggs v. Duke Power Co., 1971.

a. A4e
b. A Stake in the Outcome
c. AAAI
d. Adverse impact

18. _________, commonly known as e-commerce, consists of the buying and selling of products or services over electronic systems such as the Internet and other computer networks. The amount of trade conducted electronically has grown extraordinarily with widespread Internet usage. The use of commerce is conducted in this way, spurring and drawing on innovations in electronic funds transfer, supply chain management, Internet marketing, online transaction processing, electronic data interchange (EDI), inventory management systems, and automated data collection systems.

a. A4e
b. A Stake in the Outcome
c. Online shopping
d. Electronic commerce

19. In economics, the people in the _________ are the suppliers of labor. The _________ is all the nonmilitary people who are employed or unemployed. In 2005, the worldwide _________ was over 3 billion people.

a. Labor force
b. Pink-collar worker
c. Decent work
d. Departmentalization

20. While the full name of the Swiss verein is Deloitte Touche Tohmatsu, in 1989 it initially branded itself _________ and then simply Deloitte. In 2003 the rebranding campaign was commissioned by Bill Parrett, the then CEO of DTT, and led by Jerry Leamon, the global Clients and Markets leader.

Deloitte member firms offer services in the following functions, with country-specific variations on their legal implementation (i.e. all operating within a single company or through separate legal entities operating as subsidiaries of an umbrella legal entity for the country.)

a. 1990 Clean Air Act
b. 28-hour day
c. 33 Strategies of War
d. Deloitte ' Touche

21. In economics, the term _________ refers to situations where the advancement of a qualified person within the hierarchy of an organization is stopped at a lower level because of some form of discrimination, most commonly sexism or racism, but since the term was coined, '_________' has also come to describe the limited advancement of the deaf, blind, disabled, aged and sexual minorities.It is an unofficial, invisible barrier that prevents women and minorities from advancing in businesses.

This situation is referred to as a 'ceiling' as there is a limitation blocking upward advancement, and 'glass' (transparent) because the limitation is not immediately apparent and is normally an unwritten and unofficial policy. This invisible barrier continues to exist, even though there are no explicit obstacles keeping minorities from acquiring advanced job positions - there are no advertisements that specifically say 'no minorities hired at this establishment', nor are there any formal orders that say 'minorities are not qualified' - but they do lie beneath the surface.

a. 28-hour day
b. 1990 Clean Air Act
c. 33 Strategies of War
d. Glass Ceiling

22. The 'business case for _________', theorizes that in a global marketplace, a company that employs a diverse workforce (both men and women, people of many generations, people from ethnically and racially diverse backgrounds etc.) is better able to understand the demographics of the marketplace it serves and is thus better equipped to thrive in that marketplace than a company that has a more limited range of employee demographics.

An additional corollary suggests that a company that supports the _________ of its workforce can also improve employee satisfaction, productivity and retention.

a. Virtual team
b. Trademark
c. Kanban
d. Diversity

23. The _________ is the labour pool in employment. It is generally used to describe those working for a single company or industry, but can also apply to a geographic region like a city, country, state, etc. The term generally excludes the employers or management, and implies those involved in manual labour.

a. Pink-collar worker
b. Work-life balance
c. Division of labour
d. Workforce

24. _________ was a writer, management consultant, and self-described 'social ecologist.' Widely considered to be 'the father of modern management,' his 39 books and countless scholarly and popular articles explored how humans are organized across all sectors of society--in business, government and the nonprofit world. His writings have predicted many of the major developments of the late twentieth century, including privatization and decentralization; the rise of Japan to economic world power; the decisive importance of marketing; and the emergence of the information society with its necessity of lifelong learning. In 1959, Drucker coined the term 'knowledge worker' and later in his life considered knowledge work productivity to be the next frontier of management.

a. Jacques Al-Salawat Nasruddin Nasser
b. Debora L. Spar
c. Chrissie Hynde
d. Peter Ferdinand Drucker

25. _________ is an advertisement in which a particular product specifically mentions a competitor by name for the express purpose of showing why the competitor is inferior to the product naming it.

This should not be confused with parody advertisements, where a fictional product is being advertised for the purpose of poking fun at the particular advertisement, nor should it be confused with the use of a coined brand name for the purpose of comparing the product without actually naming an actual competitor. ('Wikipedia tastes better and is less filling than the Encyclopedia Galactica.')

In the 1980s, during what has been referred to as the cola wars, soft-drink manufacturer Pepsi ran a series of advertisements where people, caught on hidden camera, in a blind taste test, chose Pepsi over rival Coca-Cola.

a. 1990 Clean Air Act
b. 33 Strategies of War
c. 28-hour day
d. Comparative advertising

26. An arbitral tribunal (or arbitration tribunal) is a panel of one or more adjudicators which is convened and sits to resolve a dispute by way of arbitration. The tribunal may consist of a sole _________, or there may be two or more _________s, which might include either a chairman or an umpire. The parties to a dispute are usually free to agree the number and composition of the arbitral tribunal.

a. Arbitrator
b. AAAI
c. A Stake in the Outcome
d. A4e

27. In organized labor, _________ is the method whereby workers organize together (usually in unions) to meet, converse, and negotiate upon the work conditions with their employers normally resulting in a written contract setting forth the wages, hours, and other conditions to be observed for a stipulated period.It is the practice in which union and company representatives meet to negotiate a new labor contract. In various national labor and employment law contexts, the term _________ takes on a more specific legal meaning. In a broad sense, however, it is the coming together of workers to negotiate their employment.

a. Collective bargaining
b. Paid time off
c. Labor rights
d. Labour law

28. _________ is an increasingly broadening term with which an organization, or other human system describes the combination of traditionally administrative personnel functions with acquisition and application of skills, knowledge and experience, Employee Relations and resource planning at various levels. The field draws upon concepts developed in Industrial/Organizational Psychology and System Theory. _________ has at least two related interpretations depending on context. The original usage derives from political economy and economics, where it was traditionally called labor, one of four factors of production although this perspective is changing as a function of new and ongoing research into more strategic approaches at national levels. This first usage is used more in terms of '_________ development', and can go beyond just organizations to the level of nations . The more traditional usage within corporations and businesses refers to the individuals within a firm or agency, and to the portion of the organization that deals with hiring, firing, training, and other personnel issues, typically referred to as `_________ management'.

a. Bradford Factor
b. Human resources
c. Human resource management
d. Progressive discipline

29. _________ refers to various methodologies for analyzing the requirements of a job.

The general purpose of _________ is to document the requirements of a job and the work performed. Job and task analysis is performed as a basis for later improvements, including: definition of a job domain; describing a job; developing performance appraisals, selection systems, promotion criteria, training needs assessment, and compensation plans.

a. Job analysis
b. Management process
c. Work design
d. Hersey-Blanchard situational theory

30. A _________ is a list of the general tasks and responsibilities of a position. Typically, it also includes to whom the position reports, specifications such as the qualifications needed by the person in the job, salary range for the position, etc. A _________ is usually developed by conducting a job analysis, which includes examining the tasks and sequences of tasks necessary to perform the job.

a. Recruitment
b. Recruitment advertising
c. Job description
d. Recruitment Process Insourcing

31. _________ is the process of estimation in unknown situations. Prediction is a similar, but more general term. Both can refer to estimation of time series, cross-sectional or longitudinal data.

a. 28-hour day
b. Forecasting
c. 33 Strategies of War
d. 1990 Clean Air Act

32. _________ refers to the process of screening, and selecting qualified people for a job at an organization or firm mid- and large-size organizations and companies often retain professional recruiters or outsource some of the process to _________ agencies. External _________ is the process of attracting and selecting employees from outside the organization.

The _________ industry has four main types of agencies: employment agencies, _________ websites and job search engines, 'headhunters' for executive and professional _________, and in-house _________.

a. Recruitment Process Outsourcing
b. Recruitment
c. Labour hire
d. Referral recruitment

33. _________ is the temporary suspension or permanent termination of employment of an employee or (more commonly) a group of employees for business reasons, such as the decision that certain positions are no longer necessary or a business slow-down or interruption in work. Originally the term '_________' referred exclusively to a temporary interruption in work, as when factory work cyclically falls off. However, in recent times the term can also refer to the permanent elimination of a position.

a. Retirement
b. Wrongful dismissal
c. Termination of employment
d. Layoff

34. The U.S. _________ is an independent agency of the United States government which holds primary responsibility for enforcing the federal securities laws and regulating the securities industry, the nation's stock and options exchanges, and other electronic securities markets. The SEC was created by section 4 of the Securities Exchange Act of 1934 (now codified as 15 U.S.C. Â§ 78d and commonly referred to as the 1934 Act.)

a. 28-hour day
b. 1990 Clean Air Act
c. 33 Strategies of War
d. Securities and Exchange Commission

35. A _________ or background investigation is the process of looking up and compiling criminal records, commercial records and financial records (in certain instances such as employment screening) of an individual.

_________s are often requested by employers on job candidates, especially on candidates seeking a position that requires high security or a position of trust, such as in a school, hospital, financial institution, airport, and government (including law enforcement and military.) These checks are traditionally administered by a government agency for a nominal fee, but can also be administered by private companies.

a. Labour productivity
b. Time and attendance
c. Background check
d. Malcolm Baldrige National Quality Award

36. _________ is a business management strategy aimed at embedding awareness of quality in all organizational processes. _________ has been widely used in manufacturing, education, hospitals, call centers, government, and service industries, as well as NASA space and science programs.

As defined by the International Organization for Standardization (ISO):

> '_________ is a management approach for an organization, centered on quality, based on the participation of all its members and aiming at long-term success through customer satisfaction, and benefits to all members of the organization and to society.' ISO 8402:1994

One major aim is to reduce variation from every process so that greater consistency of effort is obtained. (Royse, D., Thyer, B., Padgett D., ' Logan T., 2006)

a. 1990 Clean Air Act
b. 28-hour day
c. Quality management
d. Total quality management

37. In the field of human resource management, _________ is the field concerned with organizational activity aimed at bettering the performance of individuals and groups in organizational settings. It has been known by several names, including employee development, human resource development, and learning and development.

Harrison observes that the name was endlessly debated by the Chartered Institute of Personnel and Development during its review of professional standards in 1999/2000.

a. Training and development
b. Person specification
c. Revolving door syndrome
d. Performance appraisal

38. _________ is an approach to management development where an individual is moved through a schedule of assignments designed to give him or her a breadth of exposure to the entire operation.

_________ is also practiced to allow qualified employees to gain more insights into the processes of a company, and to reduce boredom and increase job satisfaction through job variation.

The term _________ can also mean the scheduled exchange of persons in offices, especially in public offices, prior to the end of incumbency or the legislative period.

a. 28-hour day
b. 1990 Clean Air Act
c. 33 Strategies of War
d. Job rotation

39. _________ is a method by which the job performance of an employee is evaluated _________ is a part of career development.

_________s are regular reviews of employee performance within organizations

Generally, the aims of a _________ are to:

- Give feedback on performance to employees.
- Identify employee training needs.
- Document criteria used to allocate organizational rewards.
- Form a basis for personnel decisions: salary increases, promotions, disciplinary actions, etc.
- Provide the opportunity for organizational diagnosis and development.
- Facilitate communication between employee and administraton
- Validate selection techniques and human resource policies to meet federal Equal Employment Opportunity requirements.

A common approach to assessing performance is to use a numerical or scalar rating system whereby managers are asked to score an individual against a number of objectives/attributes. In some companies, employees receive assessments from their manager, peers, subordinates and customers while also performing a self assessment.

a. Progressive discipline
b. Personnel management
c. Human resource management
d. Performance appraisal

40. In psychology research on behaviorism, _________ are scales used to report performance. _________ are normally presented vertically with scale points ranging from five to nine.

It is an appraisal method that aims to combine the benefits of narratives, critical incident incidents, and quantified ratings by anchoring a quantified scale with specific narrative examples of good or poor performance.

a. 1990 Clean Air Act
b. 33 Strategies of War
c. 28-hour day
d. Behaviorally anchored rating scales

41. A _________ is a set of categories designed to elicit information about a quantitative or a qualitative attribute. In the social sciences, common examples are the Likert scale and 1-10 _________s in which a person selects the number which is considered to reflect the perceived quality of a product.

A _________ is an instrument that requires the rater to assign the rated object that have numerals assigned to them.

a. Spearman-Brown prediction formula
b. Polytomous Rasch model
c. Rating scale
d. Thurstone scale

42. _________ refers to increasing the spiritual, political, social or economic strength of individuals and communities. It often involves the empowered developing confidence in their own capacities.

The term Human _________ covers a vast landscape of meanings, interpretations, definitions and disciplines ranging from psychology and philosophy to the highly commercialized Self-Help industry and Motivational sciences.

a. Empowerment
b. A Stake in the Outcome
c. A4e
d. AAAI

43. _________ has been described as the 'process of social influence in which one person can enlist the aid and support of others in the accomplishment of a common task' . A definition more inclusive of followers comes from Alan Keith of Genentech who said '_________ is ultimately about creating a way for people to contribute to making something extraordinary happen.'

_________ is one of the most salient aspects of the organizational context. However, defining _________ has been challenging.

a. Situational leadership
b. 28-hour day
c. Leadership
d. 1990 Clean Air Act

44. The _________ Automobile Company is an automobile manufacturer based in Wolfsburg, Germany, and is the original brand within the _________ Group, as well as the largest brand by sales volume.

_________ means 'people's car' in German, in which it is pronounced . Its current tagline or slogan is Das Auto .

a. Turnover
b. Competence-based Strategic Management
c. Rate of return
d. Volkswagen

45. _________ is a term used to describe the lifestyle of women who choose to leave the workforce (typically in white collar career positions) in order to pursue childbearing. This is the converse of the Fast Track, where one devotes considerable energy to career building.

This is a source of considerable political and social discussion.

a. 1990 Clean Air Act
b. 28-hour day
c. 33 Strategies of War
d. Mommy track

46. An _________ is an interview conducted by an employer of a departing employee. They are generally conducted by a relatively neutral party, such as a human resources staff member, so that the employee will be more inclined to be candid, as opposed to worrying about burning bridges. For this reason, some companies opt to employ a third party to conduct the interviews and provide feedback.

a. Extra role performance
b. Occupational Employment Statistics
c. Exit interview
d. Underemployment

47. The _________ of 1938 (_________, ch. 676, 52 Stat. 1060, June 25, 1938, 29 U.S.C. ch.8), also called the Wages and Hours Bill, is United States federal law that applies to employees engaged in interstate commerce or employed by an enterprise engaged in commerce or in the production of goods for commerce, unless the employer can claim an exemption from coverage. The _________ established a national minimum wage, guaranteed time and a half for overtime in certain jobs, and prohibited most employment of minors in 'oppressive child labor,' a term defined in the statute.

a. Fair Labor Standards Act
b. Board of directors
c. Joint venture
d. Family and Medical Leave Act of 1993

48. _________ are conventions, treaties and recommendations designed to eliminate unjust and inhumane labour practices. The primary inernational agency charged with developing such standards is the International Labour Organization (ILO.) Established in 1919, the ILO advocates international standards as essential for the eradication of labour conditions involving 'injustice, hardship and privation'.

a. Anaconda Copper
b. Airbus SAS
c. Airbus Industrie
d. International labour standards

49. _________ is the process of systematically determining a relative value of jobs in an organisation. In all cases the idea is to evaluate the job, not the person doing it.

- Job Ranking is the most simple form. Basically you just order the jobs according to perceived seniority. It's easy in a small organization, but get exponentially difficult with lots of different jobs.

- Pair Comparison introduces more rigour by comparing jobs in pairs, but really it's a more structured way of building a basic rank order.

- Benchmarking or slotting sets up certain jobs that are analysed in detail. These are then used for comparison to slot jobs against these benchmarks.

a. Job evaluation
b. 28-hour day
c. 33 Strategies of War
d. 1990 Clean Air Act

50. A _________ is a compensation, usually financial, received by a worker in exchange for their labor.

Compensation in terms of _________s is given to worker and compensation in terms of salary is given to employees. Compensation is a monetary benefits given to employees in returns of the services provided by them.

a. Profit-sharing agreement
b. Performance-related pay
c. State Compensation Insurance Fund
d. Wage

51. _________ is how top executives of business corporations are paid. This includes a basic salary, bonuses, shares, options and other company benefits. Over the past three decades, _________ has risen dramatically beyond the rising levels of an average worker's wage.

a. Evidence-based management
b. Anti-leadership
c. Association management company
d. Executive compensation

1. The _________ was a period in the late 18th and early 19th centuries when major changes in agriculture, manufacturing, mining, and transportation had a profound effect on the socioeconomic and cultural conditions in Britain. The changes subsequently spread throughout Europe, North America, and eventually the world. The onset of the _________ marked a major turning point in human society; almost every aspect of daily life was eventually influenced in some way.

a. Industrial Revolution
b. Affiliation
c. Abraham Harold Maslow
d. Adam Smith

2. _________ describes the situation when output from (or information about the result of) an event or phenomenon in the past will influence the same event/phenomenon in the present or future. When an event is part of a chain of cause-and-effect that forms a circuit or loop, then the event is said to 'feed back' into itself.

_________ is also a synonym for:

- _________ signal; the information about the initial event that is the basis for subsequent modification of the event.
- _________ loop; the causal path that leads from the initial generation of the _________ signal to the subsequent modification of the event.

_________ is a mechanism, process or signal that is looped back to control a system within itself. Such a loop is called a _________ loop.

a. Feedback loop
b. 1990 Clean Air Act
c. Feedback
d. Positive feedback

3. _________ is one of the managerial functions like planning, organizing, staffing and directing. It is an important function because it helps to check the errors and to take the corrective action so that deviation from standards are minimized and stated goals of the organization are achieved in desired manner.According to modern concepts, _________ is a foreseeing action whereas earlier concept of _________ was used only when errors were detected. _________ in management means setting standards, measuring actual performance and taking corrective action.

a. Schedule of reinforcement
b. Turnover
c. Decision tree pruning
d. Control

4. _________, commonly known as e-commerce, consists of the buying and selling of products or services over electronic systems such as the Internet and other computer networks. The amount of trade conducted electronically has grown extraordinarily with widespread Internet usage. The use of commerce is conducted in this way, spurring and drawing on innovations in electronic funds transfer, supply chain management, Internet marketing, online transaction processing, electronic data interchange (EDI), inventory management systems, and automated data collection systems.

a. Online shopping
b. A4e
c. Electronic commerce
d. A Stake in the Outcome

5. _________ is a form of communication that typically attempts to persuade potential customers to purchase or to consume more of a particular brand of product or service. 'While now central to the contemporary global economy and the reproduction of global production networks, it is only quite recently that _________ has been more than a marginal influence on patterns of sales and production. The formation of modern _________ was intimately bound up with the emergence of new forms of monopoly capitalism around the end of the 19th and beginning of the 20th century as one element in corporate strategies to create, organize and where possible control markets, especially for mass produced consumer goods.

a. A Stake in the Outcome
b. AAAI
c. A4e
d. Advertising

6. _________ can be regarded as an outcome of mental processes (cognitive process) leading to the selection of a course of action among several alternatives. Every _________ process produces a final choice. The output can be an action or an opinion of choice.

a. 1990 Clean Air Act
b. 33 Strategies of War
c. 28-hour day
d. Decision making

7. _________ is decision making in groups consisting of multiple members/entities. The challenge of group decision is deciding what action a group should take. There are various systems designed to solve this problem.

a. Genbutsu
b. Control of Substances Hazardous to Health Regulations 2002
c. Collaborative Planning, Forecasting and Replenishment
d. Groups decision making

8. The U.S. _________ is an independent agency of the United States government which holds primary responsibility for enforcing the federal securities laws and regulating the securities industry, the nation's stock and options exchanges, and other electronic securities markets. The SEC was created by section 4 of the Securities Exchange Act of 1934 (now codified as 15 U.S.C. Â§ 78d and commonly referred to as the 1934 Act.)

a. 1990 Clean Air Act
b. 28-hour day
c. 33 Strategies of War
d. Securities and Exchange Commission

9. In economics, the term _________ refers to situations where the advancement of a qualified person within the hierarchy of an organization is stopped at a lower level because of some form of discrimination, most commonly sexism or racism, but since the term was coined, '_________' has also come to describe the limited advancement of the deaf, blind, disabled, aged and sexual minorities.It is an unofficial, invisible barrier that prevents women and minorities from advancing in businesses.

This situation is referred to as a 'ceiling' as there is a limitation blocking upward advancement, and 'glass' (transparent) because the limitation is not immediately apparent and is normally an unwritten and unofficial policy. This invisible barrier continues to exist, even though there are no explicit obstacles keeping minorities from acquiring advanced job positions - there are no advertisements that specifically say 'no minorities hired at this establishment', nor are there any formal orders that say 'minorities are not qualified' - but they do lie beneath the surface.

a. 33 Strategies of War
b. 1990 Clean Air Act
c. 28-hour day
d. Glass Ceiling

10. The 'business case for _________', theorizes that in a global marketplace, a company that employs a diverse workforce (both men and women, people of many generations, people from ethnically and racially diverse backgrounds etc.) is better able to understand the demographics of the marketplace it serves and is thus better equipped to thrive in that marketplace than a company that has a more limited range of employee demographics.

An additional corollary suggests that a company that supports the _________ of its workforce can also improve employee satisfaction, productivity and retention.

a. Trademark
b. Diversity
c. Virtual team
d. Kanban

11. _________ is unwelcome harassment of a sexual nature, or based upon the receiving party's sex or gender. In some contexts or circumstances, _________ may be illegal. It includes a range of behavior from seemingly mild transgressions and annoyances to actual sexual abuse or sexual assault.

a. 28-hour day
b. 1990 Clean Air Act
c. Hypernorms
d. Sexual harassment

12. _________ has been described as the 'process of social influence in which one person can enlist the aid and support of others in the accomplishment of a common task' . A definition more inclusive of followers comes from Alan Keith of Genentech who said '_________ is ultimately about creating a way for people to contribute to making something extraordinary happen.'

_________ is one of the most salient aspects of the organizational context. However, defining _________ has been challenging.

a. 1990 Clean Air Act
b. 28-hour day
c. Situational leadership
d. Leadership

13. _________ or lean production, which is often known simply as 'Lean', is a production practice that considers the expenditure of resources for any goal other than the creation of value for the end customer to be wasteful, and thus a target for elimination. Working from the perspective of the customer who consumes a product or service, 'value' is defined as any action or process that a customer would be willing to pay for. Basically, lean is centered around creating more value with less work.

a. Theory of constraints
b. Six Sigma
c. Production line
d. Lean Manufacturing

14. _________ is a concept related to lean and just-in-time (JIT) production. The Japanese word _________ is a common term meaning 'signboard' or 'billboard'. According to Taiichi Ohno, the man credited with developing JIT, _________ is a means through which JIT is achieved.

a. Kanban
b. Succession planning
c. Trademark
d. Risk management

15. _________ is an area of knowledge within organizational theory that studies models and theories about the way an organization learns and adapts.

In Organizational development (OD), learning is a characteristic of an adaptive organization, i.e., an organization that is able to sense changes in signals from its environment (both internal and external) and adapt accordingly.

a. A4e
b. A Stake in the Outcome
c. AAAI
d. Organizational learning

16. _________ is an advertisement in which a particular product specifically mentions a competitor by name for the express purpose of showing why the competitor is inferior to the product naming it.

This should not be confused with parody advertisements, where a fictional product is being advertised for the purpose of poking fun at the particular advertisement, nor should it be confused with the use of a coined brand name for the purpose of comparing the product without actually naming an actual competitor. ('Wikipedia tastes better and is less filling than the Encyclopedia Galactica.')

In the 1980s, during what has been referred to as the cola wars, soft-drink manufacturer Pepsi ran a series of advertisements where people, caught on hidden camera, in a blind taste test, chose Pepsi over rival Coca-Cola.

a. Comparative advertising
b. 28-hour day
c. 1990 Clean Air Act
d. 33 Strategies of War

1. _________ is a business management strategy aimed at embedding awareness of quality in all organizational processes. _________ has been widely used in manufacturing, education, hospitals, call centers, government, and service industries, as well as NASA space and science programs.

As defined by the International Organization for Standardization (ISO):

> '_________ is a management approach for an organization, centered on quality, based on the participation of all its members and aiming at long-term success through customer satisfaction, and benefits to all members of the organization and to society.' ISO 8402:1994

One major aim is to reduce variation from every process so that greater consistency of effort is obtained. (Royse, D., Thyer, B., Padgett D., ' Logan T., 2006)

a. 28-hour day
b. Quality management
c. 1990 Clean Air Act
d. Total quality management

2. _________ of the learning curve effect and the closely related experience curve effect express the relationship between equations for experience and efficiency or between efficiency gains and investment in the effort. The experience of 'learning curves' was first observed by the 19th Century German psychologist Hermann Ebbinghaus according to the difficulty of memorizing varying numbers of verbal stimuli, and subsequent learning about the complex processes of learning are discussed in the

.

The rule used for representing the learning curve effect states that the more times a task has been performed, the less time will be required on each subsequent iteration.

a. Point biserial correlation coefficient
b. Models
c. Spatial Decision Support Systems
d. Distribution

3. Maslow's _________ is a theory in psychology, proposed by Abraham Maslow in his 1943 paper A Theory of Human Motivation, which he subsequently extended to include his observations of humans' innate curiosity.

Maslow's _________ is predetermined in order of importance. It is often depicted as a pyramid consisting of five levels: the lowest level is associated with physiological needs, while the uppermost level is associated with self-actualization needs, particularly those related to identity and purpose. Deficiency needs must be met first. Once these are met, seeking to satisfy growth needs drives personal growth. The higher needs in this hierarchy only come into focus when the lower needs in the pyramid are met.

a. 1990 Clean Air Act
b. Hierarchy of needs
c. 33 Strategies of War
d. 28-hour day

4. _________ is the temporary suspension or permanent termination of employment of an employee or (more commonly) a group of employees for business reasons, such as the decision that certain positions are no longer necessary or a business slow-down or interruption in work. Originally the term '_________' referred exclusively to a temporary interruption in work, as when factory work cyclically falls off. However, in recent times the term can also refer to the permanent elimination of a position.

a. Retirement
b. Wrongful dismissal
c. Termination of employment
d. Layoff

5. _________ are job factors that can cause dissatisfaction if missing but do not necessarily motivate employees if increased.

_________ have mostly to do with the job environment. These factors are important or notable only when they are lacking.

a. Hygiene factors
b. Work-at-home scheme
c. Split shift
d. Work system

6. _________ was developed by Frederick Herzberg, a psychologist who found that job satisfaction and job dissatisfaction acted independently of each other. _________ states that there are certain factors in the workplace that cause job satisfaction, while a separate set of factors cause dissatisfaction.

a. Need for power
b. Two-factor theory
c. 1990 Clean Air Act
d. Need for Achievement

7. _________ refers to an individual's desire for significant accomplishment, mastering of skills, control, or high standards. The term was introduced by the psychologist, David McClelland.

_________ is related to the difficulty of tasks people choose to undertake.

a. Two-factor theory
b. Need for achievement
c. Need for power
d. 1990 Clean Air Act

8. Clayton Paul Alderfer is an American psychologist who further expanded Maslow's hierarchy of needs by categorizing the hierarchy into his _________ Alderfer categorized the lower order needs (Physiological and Safety) into the Existence category. He fit Maslow's interpersonal love and esteem needs into the relatedness category. The growth category contained the Self Actualization and self esteem needs.

Alderfer also proposed a regression theory to go along with the _________. He said that when needs in a higher category are not met then individuals redouble the efforts invested in a lower category need.

a. ERG theory
b. Adam Smith
c. Alvin Neill Jackson
d. Abraham Harold Maslow

9. The U.S. _________ is a federal agency whose goal is ending employment discrimination. The _________ investigates discrimination complaints based on an individual's race, color, national origin, religion, sex, age, disability and retaliation for reporting and/or opposing a discriminatory practice. The Commission is also tasked with filing suits on behalf of alleged victim(s) of discrimination against employers and as an adjudicatory for claims of discrimination brought against federal agencies.

a. Equal Employment Opportunity Commission
b. Airbus SAS
c. ARCO
d. Airbus Industrie

10. _________ is about the mental processes regarding choice, or choosing. It explains the processes that an individual undergoes to make choices. In organizational behavior study, _________ is a motivation theory first proposed by Victor Vroom of the Yale School of Management.

a. A Stake in the Outcome
b. A4e
c. AAAI
d. Expectancy theory

11. In operant conditioning, _________ occurs when an event following a response causes an increase in the probability of that response occurring in the future. Response strength can be assessed by measures such as the frequency with which the response is made (for example, a pigeon may peck a key more times in the session), or the speed with which it is made (for example, a rat may run a maze faster.) The environment change contingent upon the response is called a reinforcer.

a. Meetings, Incentives, Conferences, and Exhibitions
b. Historiometry
c. Reinforcement
d. Diminishing Manufacturing Sources and Material Shortages

12. _________ is an advertisement in which a particular product specifically mentions a competitor by name for the express purpose of showing why the competitor is inferior to the product naming it.

This should not be confused with parody advertisements, where a fictional product is being advertised for the purpose of poking fun at the particular advertisement, nor should it be confused with the use of a coined brand name for the purpose of comparing the product without actually naming an actual competitor. ('Wikipedia tastes better and is less filling than the Encyclopedia Galactica.')

In the 1980s, during what has been referred to as the cola wars, soft-drink manufacturer Pepsi ran a series of advertisements where people, caught on hidden camera, in a blind taste test, chose Pepsi over rival Coca-Cola.

a. Comparative advertising
b. 33 Strategies of War
c. 1990 Clean Air Act
d. 28-hour day

13. The _________ 1970 is an Act of the United Kingdom Parliament which prohibits any less favourable treatment between men and women in terms of pay and conditions of employment. It came into force on 29 December 1975. The term pay is interpreted in a broad sense to include, on top of wages, things like holidays, pension rights, company perks and some kinds of bonuses.

a. Architectural Barriers Act of 1968
b. Australian labour law
c. Oncale v. Sundowner Offshore Services
d. Equal Pay Act

14. _________ attempts to explain relational satisfaction in terms of perceptions of fair/unfair distributions of resources within interpersonal relationships. _________ is considered as one of the justice theories, It was first developed in 1962 by John Stacey Adams, a workplace and behavioral psychologist, who asserted that employees seek to maintain equity between the inputs that they bring to a job and the outcomes that they receive from it against the perceived inputs and outcomes of others (Adams, 1965.) The belief is that people value fair treatment which causes them to be motivated to keep the fairness maintained within the relationships of their co-workers and the organization.

a. Equity theory
b. A Stake in the Outcome
c. A4e
d. AAAI

15. _________ has become one of the most popular theories in organizational psychology.

Goal setting has been a formula used for acheivement since the early 1800s. The form and pattern has cahanged drastically over the years and there is still much debate as to what is the most efective pattern to follow.

a. Human relations
b. Goal-setting theory
c. Job satisfaction
d. Corporate Culture

16. _________ and Theory Y are theories of human motivation created and developed by Douglas McGregor at the MIT Sloan School of Management in the 1960s that have been used in human resource management, organizational behavior, organizational communication and organizational development. They describe two very different attitudes toward workforce motivation. McGregor felt that companies followed either one or the other approach.

In _________, which many managers practice, management assumes employees are inherently lazy and will avoid work if they can. They inherently dislike work. Because of this, workers need to be closely supervised and comprehensive systems of controls developed.

a. Theory X
b. Cash cow
c. Management team
d. Job enrichment

17. Theory X and _________ are theories of human motivation created and developed by Douglas McGregor at the MIT Sloan School of Management in the 1960s that have been used in human resource management, organizational behavior, organizational communication and organizational development. They describe two very different attitudes toward workforce motivation. McGregor felt that companies followed either one or the other approach.

In _________, management assumes employees may be ambitious and self-motivated and exercise self-control. It is believed that employees enjoy their mental and physical work duties.

a. Contingency theory
b. Business Workflow Analysis
c. Design leadership
d. Theory Y

18. An _________ is a private computer network that uses Internet technologies to securely share any part of an organization's information or operational systems with its employees. Sometimes the term refers only to the organization's internal website, but often it is a more extensive part of the organization's computer infrastructure and private websites are an important component and focal point of internal communication and collaboration.

An _________ is built from the same concepts and technologies used for the Internet, such as client-server computing and the Internet Protocol Suite (TCP/IP.)

a. A4e
b. AAAI
c. A Stake in the Outcome
d. Intranet

19. The _________ captures an expanded spectrum of values and criteria for measuring organizational success: economic, ecological and social. With the ratification of the United Nations and ICLEI _________ standard for urban and community accounting in early 2007, this became the dominant approach to public sector full cost accounting. Similar UN standards apply to natural capital and human capital measurement to assist in measurements required by _________, e.g. the ecoBudget standard for reporting ecological footprint.

a. Triple bottom line
b. 33 Strategies of War
c. 28-hour day
d. 1990 Clean Air Act

20. The 'business case for _________', theorizes that in a global marketplace, a company that employs a diverse workforce (both men and women, people of many generations, people from ethnically and racially diverse backgrounds etc.) is better able to understand the demographics of the marketplace it serves and is thus better equipped to thrive in that marketplace than a company that has a more limited range of employee demographics.

An additional corollary suggests that a company that supports the _________ of its workforce can also improve employee satisfaction, productivity and retention.

a. Kanban
b. Trademark
c. Virtual team
d. Diversity

21. _________ is the science, art and technology of enclosing or protecting products for distribution, storage, sale, and use. _________ also refers to the process of design, evaluation, and production of packages. _________ can be described as a coordinated system of preparing goods for transport, warehousing, logistics, sale, and end use.

a. Packaging
b. Supply chain
c. Wholesalers
d. Supply chain management

22. _________ is an American writer on business management practices, best-known for, In Search of Excellence (co-authored with Robert H. Waterman, Jr.)

Peters was born in Baltimore, Maryland. He went to Severn School for High School and attended Cornell University, receiving a bachelor's degree in civil engineering in 1965, and a master's degree in 1966.

a. Abraham Harold Maslow
b. Adam Smith
c. Affiliation
d. Thomas J. Peters

23. The general definition of an _________ is an evaluation of a person, organization, system, process, project or product. _________s are performed to ascertain the validity and reliability of information; also to provide an assessment of a system's internal control. The goal of an _________ is to express an opinion on the person / organization/system (etc) in question, under evaluation based on work done on a test basis.

a. Audit committee
b. Audit
c. Internal control
d. A Stake in the Outcome

24. _________ is an idea in the field of Organizational studies and management which describes the psychology, attitudes, experiences, beliefs and Values (personal and cultural values) of an organization. It has been defined as 'the specific collection of values and norms that are shared by people and groups in an organization and that control the way they interact with each other and with stakeholders outside the organization.'

This definition continues to explain organizational values also known as 'beliefs and ideas about what kinds of goals members of an organization should pursue and ideas about the appropriate kinds or standards of behavior organizational members should use to achieve these goals. From organizational values develop organizational norms, guidelines or expectations that prescribe appropriate kinds of behavior by employees in particular situations and control the behavior of organizational members towards one another.'

_________ is not the same as corporate culture.

a. Organizational development
b. Organizational effectiveness
c. Union shop
d. Organizational culture

25. In neuroscience, the _________ is a collection of brain structures which attempts to regulate and control behavior by inducing pleasurable effects.

A psychological reward is a process that reinforces behavior -- something that, when offered, causes a behavior to increase in intensity. Reward is an operational concept for describing the positive value an individual ascribes to an object, behavioral act or an internal physical state.

a. Reward system
b. 1990 Clean Air Act
c. 33 Strategies of War
d. 28-hour day

26. _________ means increasing the scope of a job through extending the range of its job duties and responsibilities. This contradicts the principles of specialisation and the division of labour whereby work is divided into small units, each of which is performed repetitively by an individual worker. Some motivational theories suggest that the boredom and alienation caused by the division of labour can actually cause efficiency to fall.

a. Centralization
b. Delayering
c. Mock interview
d. Job enlargement

27. _________ is an approach to management development where an individual is moved through a schedule of assignments designed to give him or her a breadth of exposure to the entire operation.

_________ is also practiced to allow qualified employees to gain more insights into the processes of a company, and to reduce boredom and increase job satisfaction through job variation.

The term _________ can also mean the scheduled exchange of persons in offices, especially in public offices, prior to the end of incumbency or the legislative period.

a. 33 Strategies of War
b. 28-hour day
c. 1990 Clean Air Act
d. Job rotation

28. _________ is the practice of using entrepreneurial skills without taking on the risks or accountability associated with entrepreneurial activities. It is practiced by employees within an established organization using a business model. Employees, perhaps engaged in a special project within a larger firm are supposed to behave as entrepreneurs, even though they have the resources and capabilities of the larger firm to draw upon.

a. AAAI
b. A4e
c. A Stake in the Outcome
d. Intrapreneurship

29. _________ is a variable work schedule, in contrast to traditional work arrangements requiring employees to work a standard 9am to 5pm day. Under _________, there is typically a core period of the day when employees are expected to be at work (for example, between 11 am and 3pm), while the rest of the working day is 'flexitime', in which employees can choose when they work, subject to achieving total daily, weekly or monthly hours in the region of what the employer expects, and subject to the necessary work being done.

A _________ policy allows staff to determine when they will work, while a flexplace policy allows staff to determine where they will work.

a. Bennett Amendment
b. Certificate of Incorporation
c. Flextime
d. Fiduciary

30. The legal _________ varies from nation to nation. The weekend is a part of the week usually lasting one or two days in which most paid workers do not work.

In Muslim-majority countries the legal work week in the Middle East is typically either Saturday through Wednesday , Saturday through Thursday or Sunday through Thursday as in Egypt.

a. Working Time Directive
b. Day One Christian Ministries
c. Business day
d. Workweek

1. _________ has been described as the 'process of social influence in which one person can enlist the aid and support of others in the accomplishment of a common task' . A definition more inclusive of followers comes from Alan Keith of Genentech who said '_________ is ultimately about creating a way for people to contribute to making something extraordinary happen.'

_________ is one of the most salient aspects of the organizational context. However, defining _________ has been challenging.

a. Situational leadership
b. Leadership
c. 28-hour day
d. 1990 Clean Air Act

2. The _________ was a period in the late 18th and early 19th centuries when major changes in agriculture, manufacturing, mining, and transportation had a profound effect on the socioeconomic and cultural conditions in Britain. The changes subsequently spread throughout Europe, North America, and eventually the world. The onset of the _________ marked a major turning point in human society; almost every aspect of daily life was eventually influenced in some way.

a. Affiliation
b. Industrial Revolution
c. Adam Smith
d. Abraham Harold Maslow

3. The general definition of an _________ is an evaluation of a person, organization, system, process, project or product. _________s are performed to ascertain the validity and reliability of information; also to provide an assessment of a system's internal control. The goal of an _________ is to express an opinion on the person / organization/system (etc) in question, under evaluation based on work done on a test basis.

a. A Stake in the Outcome
b. Internal control
c. Audit committee
d. Audit

4. The 'business case for _________', theorizes that in a global marketplace, a company that employs a diverse workforce (both men and women, people of many generations, people from ethnically and racially diverse backgrounds etc.) is better able to understand the demographics of the marketplace it serves and is thus better equipped to thrive in that marketplace than a company that has a more limited range of employee demographics.

An additional corollary suggests that a company that supports the _________ of its workforce can also improve employee satisfaction, productivity and retention.

a. Virtual team
b. Diversity
c. Trademark
d. Kanban

5. Organizational culture is not the same as _________. It is wider and deeper concepts, something that an organization 'is' rather than what it 'has' (according to Buchanan and Huczynski.)

_________ is the total sum of the values, customs, traditions and meanings that make a company unique.

a. Path-goal theory
b. Job analysis
c. Corporate culture
d. Work design

6. _________ refers to increasing the spiritual, political, social or economic strength of individuals and communities. It often involves the empowered developing confidence in their own capacities.

The term Human _________ covers a vast landscape of meanings, interpretations, definitions and disciplines ranging from psychology and philosophy to the highly commercialized Self-Help industry and Motivational sciences.

a. A Stake in the Outcome
b. AAAI
c. Empowerment
d. A4e

7. In decision theory and estimation theory, the _________ of an estimator, $\hat{\theta}$, of an unknown parameter of the distribution, θ, is the expected value of the loss function

$$R(\theta,\hat{\theta}) = \mathbb{E}_\theta L(\theta,\hat{\theta}) = \int L(\theta,\hat{\theta})\, dP_\theta.$$

where dP_θ is a probability measure parametrized by θ.

- For a scalar parameter θ and a quadratic loss function,

  $$L(\theta,\hat{\theta}) = (\theta - \hat{\theta})^2$$

  the _________ function becomes the mean squared error of the estimate,

  $$R(\theta,\hat{\theta}) = E_\theta(\theta - \hat{\theta})^2$$

- In density estimation, the unknown parameter is probability density itself. The loss function is typically chosen to be a norm in an appropriate function space. For example, for L^2 norm,

  $$L(f,\hat{f}) = \|f - \hat{f}\|_2^2$$

  the _________ function becomes the mean integrated squared error

  $$R(f,\hat{f}) = E\|f - \hat{f}\|^2$$

.

a. Financial modeling
b. Risk aversion
c. Linear model
d. Risk

8. _________ is the temporary suspension or permanent termination of employment of an employee or (more commonly) a group of employees for business reasons, such as the decision that certain positions are no longer necessary or a business slow-down or interruption in work. Originally the term '_________' referred exclusively to a temporary interruption in work, as when factory work cyclically falls off. However, in recent times the term can also refer to the permanent elimination of a position.

a. Layoff
b. Termination of employment
c. Retirement
d. Wrongful dismissal

9. _________ is the process of subjecting an author's scholarly work, research, or ideas to the scrutiny of others who are experts in the same field. _________ requires a community of experts in a given field, who are qualified and able to perform impartial review. Impartial review, especially of work in less narrowly defined or inter-disciplinary fields, may be difficult to accomplish; and the significance of an idea may never be widely appreciated among its contemporaries.

a. 33 Strategies of War
b. 28-hour day
c. 1990 Clean Air Act
d. Peer review

10. _________ or lean production, which is often known simply as 'Lean', is a production practice that considers the expenditure of resources for any goal other than the creation of value for the end customer to be wasteful, and thus a target for elimination. Working from the perspective of the customer who consumes a product or service, 'value' is defined as any action or process that a customer would be willing to pay for. Basically, lean is centered around creating more value with less work.

a. Production line
b. Lean Manufacturing
c. Theory of constraints
d. Six Sigma

11. _________ is individual power based on a high level of identification with, admiration of, or respect for the powerholder.

Nationalism, Patriotism, Celebrities and well-respected people are examples of _________ in effect.

_________ is one of the Five Bases of Social Power, as defined by Bertram Raven and his colleagues[1] in 1959.

a. 1990 Clean Air Act
b. 28-hour day
c. Referent power
d. 33 Strategies of War

12. _________ refers to an individual's desire for significant accomplishment, mastering of skills, control, or high standards. The term was introduced by the psychologist, David McClelland.

_________ is related to the difficulty of tasks people choose to undertake.

a. Two-factor theory
b. 1990 Clean Air Act
c. Need for power
d. Need for achievement

13. _________ and Theory Y are theories of human motivation created and developed by Douglas McGregor at the MIT Sloan School of Management in the 1960s that have been used in human resource management, organizational behavior, organizational communication and organizational development. They describe two very different attitudes toward workforce motivation. McGregor felt that companies followed either one or the other approach.

In _________, which many managers practice, management assumes employees are inherently lazy and will avoid work if they can. They inherently dislike work. Because of this, workers need to be closely supervised and comprehensive systems of controls developed.

a. Theory X
b. Job enrichment
c. Cash cow
d. Management team

14. Theory X and _________ are theories of human motivation created and developed by Douglas McGregor at the MIT Sloan School of Management in the 1960s that have been used in human resource management, organizational behavior, organizational communication and organizational development. They describe two very different attitudes toward workforce motivation. McGregor felt that companies followed either one or the other approach.

In _________, management assumes employees may be ambitious and self-motivated and exercise self-control. It is believed that employees enjoy their mental and physical work duties.

a. Business Workflow Analysis
b. Design leadership
c. Contingency theory
d. Theory Y

15. The _________ captures an expanded spectrum of values and criteria for measuring organizational success: economic, ecological and social. With the ratification of the United Nations and ICLEI _________ standard for urban and community accounting in early 2007, this became the dominant approach to public sector full cost accounting. Similar UN standards apply to natural capital and human capital measurement to assist in measurements required by _________, e.g. the ecoBudget standard for reporting ecological footprint.

a. 1990 Clean Air Act
b. 33 Strategies of War
c. 28-hour day
d. Triple bottom line

16. Contingency leadership theory in organizational studies is a type of leadership theory, leadership style, and leadership model that presumes that different leadership styles are contingent to different situations. It is also referred as _________ Â® theory although, as originally convened, the situational theory term is much more restrictive. The original situational theory argues that the best type of leadership is totally determined by the situational variables.Currently there are many styles of leadership.

a. 28-hour day
b. 1990 Clean Air Act
c. Situational leadership
d. Situational theory

17. The _________ is a leadership theory in the field of organizational studies developed by Robert House in 1971 and revised in 1996. The theory that a leader's behavior is contingent to the satisfaction, motivation and performance of subordinates. The revised version also argues that the leader engage in behaviors that complement subordinate's abilities and compensate for deficiencies.

a. Sociotechnical systems
b. Human relations
c. Corporate Culture
d. Path-goal theory

18. _________ is about the mental processes regarding choice, or choosing. It explains the processes that an individual undergoes to make choices. In organizational behavior study, _________ is a motivation theory first proposed by Victor Vroom of the Yale School of Management.

a. AAAI
b. A4e
c. Expectancy theory
d. A Stake in the Outcome

1. The U.S. _________ is a federal agency whose goal is ending employment discrimination. The _________ investigates discrimination complaints based on an individual's race, color, national origin, religion, sex, age, disability and retaliation for reporting and/or opposing a discriminatory practice. The Commission is also tasked with filing suits on behalf of alleged victim(s) of discrimination against employers and as an adjudicatory for claims of discrimination brought against federal agencies.

a. ARCO
b. Airbus Industrie
c. Airbus SAS
d. Equal Employment Opportunity Commission

2. A _________ is a group of employees from various functional areas of the organization - research, engineering, marketing, finance. human resources, and operations, for example - who are all focused on a specific objective and are responsible to work as a team to improve coordination and innovation across divisions and resolve mutual problems.

a. Goal-setting theory
b. Graduate recruitment
c. Sociotechnical systems
d. Cross-functional team

3. In business and engineering, new _________ is the term used to describe the complete process of bringing a new product or service to market. There are two parallel paths involved in the NProduct development process: one involves the idea generation, product design, and detail engineering; the other involves market research and marketing analysis. Companies typically see new _________ as the first stage in generating and commercializing new products within the overall strategic process of product life cycle management used to maintain or grow their market share.

a. 1990 Clean Air Act
b. Product development
c. 28-hour day
d. 33 Strategies of War

4. _________ is a business management strategy aimed at embedding awareness of quality in all organizational processes. _________ has been widely used in manufacturing, education, hospitals, call centers, government, and service industries, as well as NASA space and science programs.

As defined by the International Organization for Standardization (ISO):

> '_________ is a management approach for an organization, centered on quality, based on the participation of all its members and aiming at long-term success through customer satisfaction, and benefits to all members of the organization and to society.' ISO 8402:1994

One major aim is to reduce variation from every process so that greater consistency of effort is obtained. (Royse, D., Thyer, B., Padgett D., ' Logan T., 2006)

a. 1990 Clean Air Act
b. 28-hour day
c. Quality management
d. Total quality management

5. _________ refers to the movement of cash into or out of a business or financial product. It is usually measured during a specified, finite period of time. Measurement of _________ can be used

- to determine a project's rate of return or value. The time of _________s into and out of projects are used as inputs in financial models such as internal rate of return, and net present value.
- to determine problems with a business's liquidity. Being profitable does not necessarily mean being liquid. A company can fail because of a shortage of cash, even while profitable.
- as an alternate measure of a business's profits when it is believed that accrual accounting concepts do not represent economic realities. For example, a company may be notionally profitable but generating little operational cash (as may be the case for a company that barters its products rather than selling for cash.) In such a case, the company may be deriving additional operating cash by issuing shares evaluating default risk, re-investment requirements, etc.

_________ is a generic term used differently depending on the context. It may be defined by users for their own purposes.

a. Gross profit margin
b. Sweat equity
c. Gross profit
d. Cash flow

6. A _________ is a volunteer group composed of workers (or even students), usually under the leadership of their supervisor (but they can elect a team leader), who are trained to identify, analyse and solve work-related problems and present their solutions to management in order to improve the performance of the organization, and motivate and enrich the work of employees. When matured, true _________s become self-managing, having gained the confidence of management. _________s are an alternative to the dehumanising concept of the Division of Labour, where workers or individuals are treated like robots.

a. Certified in Production and Inventory Management
b. Quality circle
c. Competency-based job descriptions
d. Connectionist expert systems

7. A _________ -- also known as a geographically dispersed team -- is a group of individuals who work across time, space, and organizational boundaries with links strengthened by webs of communication technology. They have complementary skills and are committed to a common purpose, have interdependent performance goals, and share an approach to work for which they hold themselves mutually accountable. Geographically dispersed teams allow organizations to hire and retain the best people regardless of location.

a. Kanban
b. Trademark
c. Virtual team
d. Risk management

8. _________, commonly known as e-commerce, consists of the buying and selling of products or services over electronic systems such as the Internet and other computer networks. The amount of trade conducted electronically has grown extraordinarily with widespread Internet usage. The use of commerce is conducted in this way, spurring and drawing on innovations in electronic funds transfer, supply chain management, Internet marketing, online transaction processing, electronic data interchange (EDI), inventory management systems, and automated data collection systems.

a. Electronic commerce
b. Online shopping
c. A Stake in the Outcome
d. A4e

9. _________ is the self-government of a nation, country or some portion thereof, generally exercising sovereignty.

The term _________ is used in contrast to subjugation, which refers to a region as a 'territory' --subject to the political and military control of an external government. The word is sometimes used in a weaker sense to contrast with hegemony, the indirect control of one nation by another, more powerful nation.

a. A4e
b. AAAI
c. A Stake in the Outcome
d. Independence

10. A _________ is directly responsible for managing the day-to-day operations (and profitability) of a company.

Chief Executive Officer (CEO)

- As the top manager, the CEO is typically responsible for the entire operations of the corporation and reports directly to the chairman and board of directors. It is the CEO's responsibility to implement board decisions and initiatives and to maintain the smooth operation of the firm, with the assistance of senior management.

a. Field service management
b. Management team
c. Vorstand
d. Getting Things Done

11. The U.S. _________ is an independent agency of the United States government which holds primary responsibility for enforcing the federal securities laws and regulating the securities industry, the nation's stock and options exchanges, and other electronic securities markets. The SEC was created by section 4 of the Securities Exchange Act of 1934 (now codified as 15 U.S.C. Â§ 78d and commonly referred to as the 1934 Act.)

a. 33 Strategies of War
b. 1990 Clean Air Act
c. 28-hour day
d. Securities and Exchange Commission

12. _________ was a writer, management consultant, and self-described 'social ecologist.' Widely considered to be 'the father of modern management,' his 39 books and countless scholarly and popular articles explored how humans are organized across all sectors of society--in business, government and the nonprofit world. His writings have predicted many of the major developments of the late twentieth century, including privatization and decentralization; the rise of Japan to economic world power; the decisive importance of marketing; and the emergence of the information society with its necessity of lifelong learning. In 1959, Drucker coined the term 'knowledge worker' and later in his life considered knowledge work productivity to be the next frontier of management.

a. Jacques Al-Salawat Nasruddin Nasser
b. Chrissie Hynde
c. Debora L. Spar
d. Peter Ferdinand Drucker

13. _________ is a civil designation for persons who are incorporated in a fixed or permanent way to a society or group: regular member of the working staff, permanent staff distinguished from a supernumerary.

The term '_________' and its counterpart, 'supernumerary,' originated in Spanish and Latin American academy and government; it is now also used in countries all over the world, such as France, the U.S., England, Italy, etc.

There are _________ members of surgical organizations, of universities, of gastronomical associations, etc.

a. Affiliation
b. Abraham Harold Maslow
c. Numerary
d. Adam Smith

14. The 'business case for _________', theorizes that in a global marketplace, a company that employs a diverse workforce (both men and women, people of many generations, people from ethnically and racially diverse backgrounds etc.) is better able to understand the demographics of the marketplace it serves and is thus better equipped to thrive in that marketplace than a company that has a more limited range of employee demographics.

An additional corollary suggests that a company that supports the _________ of its workforce can also improve employee satisfaction, productivity and retention.

a. Kanban
b. Virtual team
c. Diversity
d. Trademark

15. _________ is the term used to describe a situation where different entities cooperate advantageously for a final outcome. Simply defined, it means that the whole is greater than the sum of the individual parts. Although the whole will be greater than each individual part, this is not the concept of _________.

a. 1990 Clean Air Act
b. 28-hour day
c. 33 Strategies of War
d. Synergy

16. In economics, business, retail, and accounting, a _________ is the value of money that has been used up to produce something, and hence is not available for use anymore. In economics, a _________ is an alternative that is given up as a result of a decision. In business, the _________ may be one of acquisition, in which case the amount of money expended to acquire it is counted as _________.

a. Fixed costs
b. Cost
c. Cost allocation
d. Cost overrun

17. _________ is the temporary suspension or permanent termination of employment of an employee or (more commonly) a group of employees for business reasons, such as the decision that certain positions are no longer necessary or a business slow-down or interruption in work. Originally the term '_________' referred exclusively to a temporary interruption in work, as when factory work cyclically falls off. However, in recent times the term can also refer to the permanent elimination of a position.

a. Termination of employment
b. Layoff
c. Retirement
d. Wrongful dismissal

18. The _________ of 1938 (_________, ch. 676, 52 Stat. 1060, June 25, 1938, 29 U.S.C. ch.8), also called the Wages and Hours Bill, is United States federal law that applies to employees engaged in interstate commerce or employed by an enterprise engaged in commerce or in the production of goods for commerce, unless the employer can claim an exemption from coverage. The _________ established a national minimum wage, guaranteed time and a half for overtime in certain jobs, and prohibited most employment of minors in 'oppressive child labor,' a term defined in the statute.

a. Family and Medical Leave Act of 1993
b. Board of directors
c. Joint venture
d. Fair Labor Standards Act

19. _________ are conventions, treaties and recommendations designed to eliminate unjust and inhumane labour practices. The primary inernational agency charged with developing such standards is the International Labour Organization (ILO.) Established in 1919, the ILO advocates international standards as essential for the eradication of labour conditions involving 'injustice, hardship and privation'.

a. Anaconda Copper
b. Airbus Industrie
c. Airbus SAS
d. International labour standards

20. _________ refers to the long-term management of intractable conflicts. It is the label for the variety of ways by which people handle grievances--standing up for what they consider to be right and against what they consider to be wrong. Those ways include such diverse phenomena as gossip, ridicule, lynching, terrorism, warfare, feuding, genocide, law, mediation, and avoidance.

a. 28-hour day
b. Conflict management
c. 33 Strategies of War
d. 1990 Clean Air Act

21. In statistics and image processing, to smooth a data set is to create an approximating function that attempts to capture important patterns in the data, while leaving out noise or other fine-scale structures/rapid phenomena. Many different algorithms are used in _________. One of the most common algorithms is the 'moving average', often used to try to capture important trends in repeated statistical surveys.

a. 33 Strategies of War
b. 28-hour day
c. 1990 Clean Air Act
d. Smoothing

22. _________ is a recursive process where two or more people or organizations work together in an intersection of common goals -- for example, an intellectual endeavor that is creative in nature--by sharing knowledge, learning and building consensus. _________ does not require leadership and can sometimes bring better results through decentralization and egalitarianism. In particular, teams that work collaboratively can obtain greater resources, recognition and reward when facing competition for finite resources._________ is also present in opposing goals exhibiting the notion of adversarial _________, though this is not a common case for using the term.

a. 28-hour day
b. 1990 Clean Air Act
c. Collectivism
d. Collaboration

23. _________ is an advertisement in which a particular product specifically mentions a competitor by name for the express purpose of showing why the competitor is inferior to the product naming it.

This should not be confused with parody advertisements, where a fictional product is being advertised for the purpose of poking fun at the particular advertisement, nor should it be confused with the use of a coined brand name for the purpose of comparing the product without actually naming an actual competitor. ('Wikipedia tastes better and is less filling than the Encyclopedia Galactica.')

In the 1980s, during what has been referred to as the cola wars, soft-drink manufacturer Pepsi ran a series of advertisements where people, caught on hidden camera, in a blind taste test, chose Pepsi over rival Coca-Cola.

a. Comparative advertising
b. 28-hour day
c. 33 Strategies of War
d. 1990 Clean Air Act

24. _________ is a business management strategy, initially implemented by Motorola, that today enjoys widespread application in many sectors of industry.

_________ seeks to improve the quality of process outputs by identifying and removing the causes of defects (errors) and variation in manufacturing and business processes. It uses a set of quality management methods, including statistical methods, and creates a special infrastructure of people within the organization ('Black Belts' etc.)

a. Takt time
b. Theory of constraints
c. Production line
d. Six Sigma

1. The _________ was a period in the late 18th and early 19th centuries when major changes in agriculture, manufacturing, mining, and transportation had a profound effect on the socioeconomic and cultural conditions in Britain. The changes subsequently spread throughout Europe, North America, and eventually the world. The onset of the _________ marked a major turning point in human society; almost every aspect of daily life was eventually influenced in some way.

a. Affiliation
b. Abraham Harold Maslow
c. Adam Smith
d. Industrial Revolution

2. _________ comprises a range of practices used in an organisation to identify, create, represent, distribute and enable adoption of insights and experiences. Such insights and experiences comprise knowledge, either embodied in individuals or embedded in organisational processes or practice.

An established discipline since 1991 , _________ includes courses taught in the fields of business administration, information systems, management, and library and information sciences .

a. 1990 Clean Air Act
b. 28-hour day
c. 33 Strategies of War
d. Knowledge management

3. _________ is a method by which the job performance of an employee is evaluated _________ is a part of career development.

_________s are regular reviews of employee performance within organizations

Generally, the aims of a _________ are to:

- Give feedback on performance to employees.
- Identify employee training needs.
- Document criteria used to allocate organizational rewards.
- Form a basis for personnel decisions: salary increases, promotions, disciplinary actions, etc.
- Provide the opportunity for organizational diagnosis and development.
- Facilitate communication between employee and administraton
- Validate selection techniques and human resource policies to meet federal Equal Employment Opportunity requirements.

A common approach to assessing performance is to use a numerical or scalar rating system whereby managers are asked to score an individual against a number of objectives/attributes. In some companies, employees receive assessments from their manager, peers, subordinates and customers while also performing a self assessment.

a. Progressive discipline
b. Human resource management
c. Performance appraisal
d. Personnel management

4. A _________ is a subset of the overall internal controls of a business covering the application of people, documents, technologies, and procedures by management accountants to solving business problems such as costing a product, service or a business-wide strategy. _________s are distinct from regular information systems in that they are used to analyze other information systems applied in operational activities in the organization. Academically, the term is commonly used to refer to the group of information management methods tied to the automation or support of human decision making, e.g. Decision Support Systems, Expert systems, and Executive information systems.

a. 1990 Clean Air Act
b. Management information system
c. 28-hour day
d. Strategic information system

5. The U.S. _________ is a federal agency whose goal is ending employment discrimination. The _________ investigates discrimination complaints based on an individual's race, color, national origin, religion, sex, age, disability and retaliation for reporting and/or opposing a discriminatory practice. The Commission is also tasked with filing suits on behalf of alleged victim(s) of discrimination against employers and as an adjudicatory for claims of discrimination brought against federal agencies.

a. Equal Employment Opportunity Commission
b. Airbus SAS
c. Airbus Industrie
d. ARCO

6. _________ is the use of computer-based software tools that assist engineers and machinists in manufacturing or prototyping product components. Its primary purpose is to create a faster production process and components with more precise dimensions and material consistency, which in some cases, uses only the required amount of raw material (thus minimizing waste), while simultaneously reducing energy consumption. CAM is a programming tool that makes it possible to manufacture physical models using computer-aided design (CAD) programs.

a. Computer-aided manufacturing
b. 33 Strategies of War
c. 1990 Clean Air Act
d. 28-hour day

7. _________, commonly known as e-commerce, consists of the buying and selling of products or services over electronic systems such as the Internet and other computer networks. The amount of trade conducted electronically has grown extraordinarily with widespread Internet usage. The use of commerce is conducted in this way, spurring and drawing on innovations in electronic funds transfer, supply chain management, Internet marketing, online transaction processing, electronic data interchange (EDI), inventory management systems, and automated data collection systems.

a. Electronic commerce
b. Online shopping
c. A4e
d. A Stake in the Outcome

8. _________ is the process of filtering for information or patterns using techniques involving collaboration among multiple agents, viewpoints, data sources, etc. Applications of _________ typically involve very large data sets. _________ methods have been applied to many different kinds of data including sensing and monitoring data - such as in mineral exploration, environmental sensing over large areas or multiple sensors; financial data - such as financial service institutions that integrate many financial sources; or in electronic commerce and web 2.0 applications where the focus is on user data, etc.

a. 1990 Clean Air Act
b. 28-hour day
c. 33 Strategies of War
d. Collaborative filtering

9. _________ is execution of a series of programs ('jobs') on a computer without human interaction.

Batch jobs are set up so they can be run to completion without human interaction, so all input data is preselected through scripts or command-line parameters. This is in contrast to 'online' or interactive programs which prompt the user for such input.

a. 33 Strategies of War
b. 28-hour day
c. 1990 Clean Air Act
d. Batch processing

10. _________ constitute a class of computer-based information systems including knowledge-based systems that support decision-making activities.

_________ are a specific class of computerized information systems that supports business and organizational decision-making activities. A properly-designed _________ is an interactive software-based system intended to help decision makers compile useful information from raw data, documents, personal knowledge, and/or business models to identify and solve problems and make decisions.

a. 1990 Clean Air Act
b. 28-hour day
c. Spatial Decision Support Systems
d. Decision support systems

11. An _________ is software that attempts to reproduce the performance of one or more human experts, most commonly in a specific problem domain, and is a traditional application and/or subfield of artificial intelligence. A wide variety of methods can be used to simulate the performance of the expert however common to most or all are 1) the creation of a so-called 'knowledgebase' which uses some knowledge representation formalism to capture the Subject Matter Experts (SME) knowledge and 2) a process of gathering that knowledge from the SME and codifying it according to the formalism, which is called knowledge engineering. _________s may or may not have learning components but a third common element is that once the system is developed it is proven by being placed in the same real world problem solving situation as the human SME, typically as an aid to human workers or a supplement to some information system.

a. A4e
b. AAAI
c. Expert system
d. A Stake in the Outcome

12. _________ is an integrated communications-based process through which individuals and communities discover that existing and newly-identified needs and wants may be satisfied by the products and services of others.

_________ is defined by the American _________ Association as the activity, set of institutions, and processes for creating, communicating, delivering, and exchanging offerings that have value for customers, clients, partners, and society at large. The term developed from the original meaning which referred literally to going to market, as in shopping, or going to a market to buy or sell goods or services.

a. Customer relationship management
b. Marketing
c. Disruptive technology
d. Market development

13. _________ is a form of communication that typically attempts to persuade potential customers to purchase or to consume more of a particular brand of product or service. 'While now central to the contemporary global economy and the reproduction of global production networks, it is only quite recently that _________ has been more than a marginal influence on patterns of sales and production. The formation of modern _________ was intimately bound up with the emergence of new forms of monopoly capitalism around the end of the 19th and beginning of the 20th century as one element in corporate strategies to create, organize and where possible control markets, especially for mass produced consumer goods.

a. AAAI
b. A4e
c. A Stake in the Outcome
d. Advertising

14. _________ is the intelligence of machines and the branch of computer science which aims to create it. Major _________ textbooks define the field as 'the study and design of intelligent agents,' where an intelligent agent is a system that perceives its environment and takes actions which maximize its chances of success. John McCarthy, who coined the term in 1956, defines it as 'the science and engineering of making intelligent machines.'

The field was founded on the claim that a central property of human beings, intelligence--the sapience of Homo sapiens--can be so precisely described that it can be simulated by a machine.

a. AAAI
b. A Stake in the Outcome
c. A4e
d. Artificial intelligence

15. _________ are a class of electronic meeting systems, a collaboration technology designed to support meetings and group work . _________ are distinct from computer supported cooperative work (CSCW) technologies as _________ are more focused on task support, whereas CSCW tools provide general communication support .

_________ were referred to as a Group Support System (GSS) or an electronic meeting system since they shared similar foundations.

a. Hoshin Kanri
b. Learning organization
c. Group decision support systems
d. 1990 Clean Air Act

16. An _________ is a type of management information system intended to facilitate and support the information and decision-making needs of senior executives by providing easy access to both internal and external information relevant to meeting the strategic goals of the organization. It is commonly considered as a specialized form of a Decision Support System (DSS)

The emphasis of _________ is on graphical displays and easy-to-use user interfaces. They offer strong reporting and drill-down capabilities.

a. A Stake in the Outcome
b. A4e
c. AAAI
d. Executive information system

17. The general definition of an _________ is an evaluation of a person, organization, system, process, project or product. _________s are performed to ascertain the validity and reliability of information; also to provide an assessment of a system's internal control. The goal of an _________ is to express an opinion on the person / organization/system (etc) in question, under evaluation based on work done on a test basis.

a. Audit
b. Audit committee
c. A Stake in the Outcome
d. Internal control

18. The 'business case for _________', theorizes that in a global marketplace, a company that employs a diverse workforce (both men and women, people of many generations, people from ethnically and racially diverse backgrounds etc.) is better able to understand the demographics of the marketplace it serves and is thus better equipped to thrive in that marketplace than a company that has a more limited range of employee demographics.

An additional corollary suggests that a company that supports the _________ of its workforce can also improve employee satisfaction, productivity and retention.

a. Virtual team
b. Diversity
c. Trademark
d. Kanban

19. _________ is subcontracting a process, such as product design or manufacturing, to a third-party company. The decision to outsource is often made in the interest of lowering cost or making better use of time and energy costs, redirecting or conserving energy directed at the competencies of a particular business, or to make more efficient use of land, labor, capital, (information) technology and resources. _________ became part of the business lexicon during the 1980s.

a. Opinion leadership
b. Operant conditioning
c. Outsourcing
d. Unemployment insurance

20. In economics, business, retail, and accounting, a _________ is the value of money that has been used up to produce something, and hence is not available for use anymore. In economics, a _________ is an alternative that is given up as a result of a decision. In business, the _________ may be one of acquisition, in which case the amount of money expended to acquire it is counted as _________.

a. Cost allocation
b. Fixed costs
c. Cost overrun
d. Cost

21. _________ is the state or fact of exclusive rights and control over property, which may be an object, land/real estate or intellectual property. An _________ right is also referred to as title. The concept of _________ has existed for thousands of years and in all cultures.

a. Emanation of the state
b. Ownership
c. A4e
d. A Stake in the Outcome

22. In economics, and cost accounting, _________ describes the total economic cost of production and is made up of variable costs, which vary according to the quantity of a good produced and include inputs such as labor and raw materials, plus fixed costs, which are independent of the quantity of a good produced and include inputs (capital) that cannot be varied in the short term, such as buildings and machinery. _________ in economics includes the total opportunity cost of each factor of production in addition to fixed and variable costs.

The rate at which _________ changes as the amount produced changes is called marginal cost.

a. 33 Strategies of War
b. 1990 Clean Air Act
c. 28-hour day
d. Total Cost

23. _________ is a financial estimate designed to help consumers and enterprise managers assess direct and indirect costs It is a form of full cost accounting.

a. 1990 Clean Air Act
b. 28-hour day
c. 33 Strategies of War
d. Total Cost of Ownership

1. _________ is one of the managerial functions like planning, organizing, staffing and directing. It is an important function because it helps to check the errors and to take the corrective action so that deviation from standards are minimized and stated goals of the organization are achieved in desired manner.According to modern concepts, _________ is a foreseeing action whereas earlier concept of _________ was used only when errors were detected. _________ in management means setting standards, measuring actual performance and taking corrective action.

a. Schedule of reinforcement
b. Decision tree pruning
c. Turnover
d. Control

2. _________ consists of the processes a company uses to track and organize its contacts with its current and prospective customers. _________ software is used to support these processes; information about customers and customer interactions can be entered, stored and accessed by employees in different company departments. Typical _________ goals are to improve services provided to customers, and to use customer contact information for targeted marketing.

a. Customer relationship management
b. Green marketing
c. Marketing plan
d. Disruptive technology

3. In decision theory and estimation theory, the _________ of an estimator, $\hat{\theta}$, of an unknown parameter of the distribution, θ, is the expected value of the loss function

$$R(\theta, \hat{\theta}) = \mathbb{E}_\theta L(\theta, \hat{\theta}) = \int L(\theta, \hat{\theta})\, dP_\theta.$$

where dP_θ is a probability measure parametrized by θ.

- For a scalar parameter θ and a quadratic loss function,

$$L(\theta, \hat{\theta}) = (\theta - \hat{\theta})^2$$

the _________ function becomes the mean squared error of the estimate,

$$R(\theta, \hat{\theta}) = E_\theta(\theta - \hat{\theta})^2$$

- In density estimation, the unknown parameter is probability density itself. The loss function is typically chosen to be a norm in an appropriate function space. For example, for L^2 norm,

$$L(f, \hat{f}) = \|f - \hat{f}\|_2^2$$

the _________ function becomes the mean integrated squared error

$$R(f, \hat{f}) = E\|f - \hat{f}\|^2$$

a. Linear model
b. Financial modeling
c. Risk aversion
d. Risk

4. A _________ is a list of the general tasks and responsibilities of a position. Typically, it also includes to whom the position reports, specifications such as the qualifications needed by the person in the job, salary range for the position, etc. A _________ is usually developed by conducting a job analysis, which includes examining the tasks and sequences of tasks necessary to perform the job.

a. Recruitment advertising
b. Job description
c. Recruitment
d. Recruitment Process Insourcing

5. _________ is a business management strategy, initially implemented by Motorola, that today enjoys widespread application in many sectors of industry.

_________ seeks to improve the quality of process outputs by identifying and removing the causes of defects (errors) and variation in manufacturing and business processes. It uses a set of quality management methods, including statistical methods, and creates a special infrastructure of people within the organization ('Black Belts' etc.)

a. Production line
b. Six Sigma
c. Theory of constraints
d. Takt time

6. _________ is a business management strategy aimed at embedding awareness of quality in all organizational processes. _________ has been widely used in manufacturing, education, hospitals, call centers, government, and service industries, as well as NASA space and science programs.

As defined by the International Organization for Standardization (ISO):

> '_________ is a management approach for an organization, centered on quality, based on the participation of all its members and aiming at long-term success through customer satisfaction, and benefits to all members of the organization and to society.' ISO 8402:1994

One major aim is to reduce variation from every process so that greater consistency of effort is obtained. (Royse, D., Thyer, B., Padgett D., ' Logan T., 2006)

a. Quality management
b. 28-hour day
c. Total quality management
d. 1990 Clean Air Act

7. _________ refers to planned and systematic production processes that provide confidence in a product's suitability for its intended purpose. Refer to the definition by Merriam-Webster for further information . It is a set of activities intended to ensure that products (goods and/or services) satisfy customer requirements in a systematic, reliable fashion.

a. 28-hour day
b. Quality assurance
c. Risk assessment
d. 1990 Clean Air Act

8. A _________ is a change implemented to address a weakness identified in a management system. Normally _________s are implemented in response to a customer complaint, abnormal levels of internal nonconformity, nonconformities identified during an internal audit or adverse or unstable trends in product and process monitoring such as would be identified by SPC.

The process of determining a _________ requires identification of actions that can be taken to prevent or mitigate the weakness.

a. Corrective action
b. 1990 Clean Air Act
c. Zero defects
d. 28-hour day

9. _________ can be regarded as an outcome of mental processes (cognitive process) leading to the selection of a course of action among several alternatives. Every _________ process produces a final choice. The output can be an action or an opinion of choice.

a. 28-hour day
b. 1990 Clean Air Act
c. 33 Strategies of War
d. Decision making

10. _________ occurs when expectant women are fired, not hired, or otherwise discriminated against due to their pregnancy or intention to become pregnant. Common forms of _________ include not being hired due to visible pregnancy or likelihood of becoming pregnant, being fired after informing an employer of one's pregnancy, being fired after maternity leave, and receiving a pay dock due to pregnancy. In the United States, since 1978, employers are legally bound to provide what insurance, leave pay, and additional support that would be bestowed upon any employee with medical leave or disability.

a. 1990 Clean Air Act
b. Pregnancy Discrimination
c. 28-hour day
d. 33 Strategies of War

11. _________ describes the situation when output from (or information about the result of) an event or phenomenon in the past will influence the same event/phenomenon in the present or future. When an event is part of a chain of cause-and-effect that forms a circuit or loop, then the event is said to 'feed back' into itself.

_________ is also a synonym for:

- _________ signal; the information about the initial event that is the basis for subsequent modification of the event.
- _________ loop; the causal path that leads from the initial generation of the _________ signal to the subsequent modification of the event.

_________ is a mechanism, process or signal that is looped back to control a system within itself. Such a loop is called a _________ loop.

a. 1990 Clean Air Act
b. Feedback loop
c. Positive feedback
d. Feedback

12. The _________ of 1967, Pub. L. No. 90-202, 81 Stat. 602 (Dec. 15, 1967), codified as Chapter 14 of Title 29 of the United States Code, 29 U.S.C. Â§ 621 through 29 U.S.C. Â§ 634 (ADEA), prohibits employment discrimination against persons 40 years of age or older in the United States). The law also sets standards for pensions and benefits provided by employers and requires that information about the needs of older workers be provided to the general public.

a. Extra time
b. Unemployment and Farm Relief Act
c. Age Discrimination in Employment Act
d. Undue hardship

13. _________ is a contract between two parties, one being the employer and the other being the employee. An employee may be defined as: 'A person in the service of another under any contract of hire, express or implied, oral or written, where the employer has the power or right to control and direct the employee in the material details of how the work is to be performed.' Black's Law Dictionary page 471 (5th ed. 1979.)

a. Exit interview
b. Employment rate
c. Employment counsellor
d. Employment

14. The 'business case for _________', theorizes that in a global marketplace, a company that employs a diverse workforce (both men and women, people of many generations, people from ethnically and racially diverse backgrounds etc.) is better able to understand the demographics of the marketplace it serves and is thus better equipped to thrive in that marketplace than a company that has a more limited range of employee demographics.

An additional corollary suggests that a company that supports the _________ of its workforce can also improve employee satisfaction, productivity and retention.

a. Virtual team
b. Kanban
c. Trademark
d. Diversity

15. In economics, the people in the _________ are the suppliers of labor. The _________ is all the nonmilitary people who are employed or unemployed. In 2005, the worldwide _________ was over 3 billion people.

a. Departmentalization
b. Decent work
c. Labor force
d. Pink-collar worker

16. The U.S. _________ is a federal agency whose goal is ending employment discrimination. The _________ investigates discrimination complaints based on an individual's race, color, national origin, religion, sex, age, disability and retaliation for reporting and/or opposing a discriminatory practice. The Commission is also tasked with filing suits on behalf of alleged victim(s) of discrimination against employers and as an adjudicatory for claims of discrimination brought against federal agencies.

a. Airbus Industrie
b. Equal Employment Opportunity Commission
c. ARCO
d. Airbus SAS

17. In economics, the term _________ refers to situations where the advancement of a qualified person within the hierarchy of an organization is stopped at a lower level because of some form of discrimination, most commonly sexism or racism, but since the term was coined, '_________' has also come to describe the limited advancement of the deaf, blind, disabled, aged and sexual minorities.It is an unofficial, invisible barrier that prevents women and minorities from advancing in businesses.

This situation is referred to as a 'ceiling' as there is a limitation blocking upward advancement, and 'glass' (transparent) because the limitation is not immediately apparent and is normally an unwritten and unofficial policy. This invisible barrier continues to exist, even though there are no explicit obstacles keeping minorities from acquiring advanced job positions - there are no advertisements that specifically say 'no minorities hired at this establishment', nor are there any formal orders that say 'minorities are not qualified' - but they do lie beneath the surface.

a. 28-hour day
b. 33 Strategies of War
c. 1990 Clean Air Act
d. Glass Ceiling

18. In the fields of science, engineering, industry and statistics, _________ is the degree of closeness of a measured or calculated quantity to its actual (true) value. _________ is closely related to precision, also called reproducibility or repeatability, the degree to which further measurements or calculations show the same or similar results. _________ indicates proximity to the true value, precision to the repeatability or reproducibility of the measurement

The results of calculations or a measurement can be accurate but not precise, precise but not accurate, neither, or both.

a. A Stake in the Outcome
b. Accuracy
c. AAAI
d. A4e

19. _________ is a variable work schedule, in contrast to traditional work arrangements requiring employees to work a standard 9am to 5pm day. Under _________, there is typically a core period of the day when employees are expected to be at work (for example, between 11 am and 3pm), while the rest of the working day is 'flexitime', in which employees can choose when they work, subject to achieving total daily, weekly or monthly hours in the region of what the employer expects, and subject to the necessary work being done.

A _________ policy allows staff to determine when they will work, while a flexplace policy allows staff to determine where they will work.

a. Fiduciary
b. Bennett Amendment
c. Certificate of Incorporation
d. Flextime

20. _________ Movement refers to those researchers of organizational development who study the behavior of people in groups, in particular workplace groups. It originated in the 1920s' Hawthorne studies, which examined the effects of social relations, motivation and employee satisfaction on factory productivity. The movement viewed workers in terms of their psychology and fit with companies, rather than as interchangeable parts.

a. Human relations
b. Hersey-Blanchard situational theory
c. Participatory management
d. Work design

21. _________ is an integrated communications-based process through which individuals and communities discover that existing and newly-identified needs and wants may be satisfied by the products and services of others.

_________ is defined by the American _________ Association as the activity, set of institutions, and processes for creating, communicating, delivering, and exchanging offerings that have value for customers, clients, partners, and society at large. The term developed from the original meaning which referred literally to going to market, as in shopping, or going to a market to buy or sell goods or services.

a. Customer relationship management
b. Market development
c. Disruptive technology
d. Marketing

22. A _________ is a subset of the overall internal controls of a business covering the application of people, documents, technologies, and procedures by management accountants to solving business problems such as costing a product, service or a business-wide strategy. _________s are distinct from regular information systems in that they are used to analyze other information systems applied in operational activities in the organization. Academically, the term is commonly used to refer to the group of information management methods tied to the automation or support of human decision making, e.g. Decision Support Systems, Expert systems, and Executive information systems.

a. Strategic information system
b. 1990 Clean Air Act
c. Management information system
d. 28-hour day

23. In business and accounting, _________s are everything of value that is owned by a person or company. Any property or object of value that one possesses, usually considered as applicable to the payment of one's debts is considered an _________. Simplistically stated, _________s are things of value that can be readily converted into cash.

a. A Stake in the Outcome
b. Asset
c. AAAI
d. A4e

24. In financial accounting, a _________ or statement of financial position is a summary of a person's or organization's balances. Assets, liabilities and ownership equity are listed as of a specific date, such as the end of its financial year. A _________ is often described as a snapshot of a company's financial condition.

a. 1990 Clean Air Act
b. 33 Strategies of War
c. Balance sheet
d. 28-hour day

25. _________ are formal records of the financial activities of a business, person, or other entity. In British English, including United Kingdom company law, _________ are often referred to as accounts, although the term _________ is also used, particularly by accountants.

_________ provide an overview of a business or person's financial condition in both short and long term.

a. 1990 Clean Air Act
b. 33 Strategies of War
c. Financial statements
d. 28-hour day

26. _________ is a company's financial statement that indicates how the revenue is transformed into the net income The purpose of the _________ is to show managers and investors whether the company made or lost money during the period being reported.

The important thing to remember about an _________ is that it represents a period of time.

a. Income statement
b. A4e
c. AAAI
d. A Stake in the Outcome

27. A mutual shareholder or _________ is an individual or company (including a corporation) that legally owns one or more shares of stock in a joint stock company. A company's shareholders collectively own that company. Thus, the typical goal of such companies is to enhance shareholder value.

a. Free riding
b. Shareholder
c. 1990 Clean Air Act
d. Stockholder

28. In finance, a _________ or accounting ratio is a ratio of two selected numerical values taken from an enterprise's financial statements. There are many standard ratios used to try to evaluate the overall financial condition of a corporation or other organization. _________s may be used by managers within a firm, by current and potential shareholders (owners) of a firm, and by a firm's creditors.

a. Return on sales
b. Financial ratio
c. Return on equity
d. Rate of return

29. Market _________ is a business, economics or investment term that refers to an asset's ability to be easily converted through an act of buying or selling without causing a significant movement in the price and with minimum loss of value. Money, or cash on hand, is the most liquid asset. An act of exchange of a less liquid asset with a more liquid asset is called liquidation.

a. 1990 Clean Air Act
b. 33 Strategies of War
c. 28-hour day
d. Liquidity

30. _________ is a financial ratio that indicates the percentage of a company's assets are provided via debt. It is the ratio of total debt (the sum of current liabilities and long-term liabilities) and total assets (the sum of current assets, fixed assets, and other assets such as 'goodwill'.)

$$\text{Debt ratio} = \frac{\text{Total Debt}}{\text{Total Assets}}$$

or alternatively:

$$\text{Debt ratio} = \frac{\text{Total Liability}}{\text{Total Assets}}$$

For example, a company with $2 million in total assets and $500,000 in total liabilities would have a _________ of 25%

Like all financial ratios, a company's _________ should be compared with their industry average or other competing firms.

a. Demand forecasting
b. 28-hour day
c. 1990 Clean Air Act
d. Debt ratio

31. The general definition of an _________ is an evaluation of a person, organization, system, process, project or product. _________s are performed to ascertain the validity and reliability of information; also to provide an assessment of a system's internal control. The goal of an _________ is to express an opinion on the person / organization/system (etc) in question, under evaluation based on work done on a test basis.

a. Internal control
b. Audit
c. Audit committee
d. A Stake in the Outcome

32. In economics, business, retail, and accounting, a _________ is the value of money that has been used up to produce something, and hence is not available for use anymore. In economics, a _________ is an alternative that is given up as a result of a decision. In business, the _________ may be one of acquisition, in which case the amount of money expended to acquire it is counted as _________.

a. Fixed costs
b. Cost allocation
c. Cost
d. Cost overrun

33. _________s are parts of a corporation that directly add to its profit.

A _________ manager is held accountable for both revenues, and costs (expenses), and therefore, profits. What this means in terms of managerial responsibilities is that the manager has to drive the sales revenue generating activities which leads to cash inflows and at the same time control the cost (cash outflows) causing activities.

a. Customer profitability
b. Process costing
c. Profit center
d. Factory overhead

34. _________ generally refers to a list of all planned expenses and revenues. It is a plan for saving and spending. A _________ is an important concept in microeconomics, which uses a _________ line to illustrate the trade-offs between two or more goods.

a. 1990 Clean Air Act
b. Budget
c. 33 Strategies of War
d. 28-hour day

35. An _________ is the annual budget of an activity stated in terms of Budget Classification Code, functional/subfunctional categories and cost accounts. It contains estimates of the total value of resources required for the performance of the operation including reimbursable work or services for others. It also includes estimates of workload in terms of total work units identified by cost accounts.

a. Expected return
b. Expected gain
c. Inflation rate
d. Operating budget

36. _________ is a technique of planning and decision-making which reverses the working process of traditional budgeting. In traditional incremental budgeting, departmental managers justify only increases over the previous year budget and what has been already spent is automatically sanctioned. No reference is made to the previous level of expenditure.

a. 33 Strategies of War
b. 28-hour day
c. 1990 Clean Air Act
d. Zero-based budgeting

37. _________s (CAPEX or capex) are expenditures creating future benefits. A _________ is incurred when a business spends money either to buy fixed assets or to add to the value of an existing fixed asset with a useful life that extends beyond the taxable year. Capex are used by a company to acquire or upgrade physical assets such as equipment, property, or industrial buildings.

a. Weighted average cost of capital
b. Capital intensive
c. 1990 Clean Air Act
d. Capital expenditure

38. In economics, _________ are business expenses that are not dependent on the activities of the business They tend to be time-related, such as salaries or rents being paid per month. This is in contrast to variable costs, which are volume-related (and are paid per quantity.)

In management accounting, _________ are defined as expenses that do not change in proportion to the activity of a business, within the relevant period or scale of production.

a. Cost allocation
b. Transaction cost
c. Cost of quality
d. Fixed costs

39. _________s are expenses that change in proportion to the activity of a business. In other words, _________ is the sum of marginal costs. It can also be considered normal costs.

a. Cost overrun
b. Cost accounting
c. Fixed costs
d. Variable cost

40. Consumer market research is a form of applied sociology that concentrates on understanding the behaviours, whims and preferences, of consumers in a market-based economy, and aims to understand the effects and comparative success of marketing campaigns. The field of consumer _________ as a statistical science was pioneered by Arthur Nielsen with the founding of the ACNielsen Company in 1923 .

Thus _________ is the systematic and objective identification, collection, analysis, and dissemination of information for the purpose of assisting management in decision making related to the identification and solution of problems and opportunities in marketing.

a. Marketing research process
b. 1990 Clean Air Act
c. Marketing research
d. Market analysis

41. _________, in strategic management and marketing is, according to Carlton O'Neal, the percentage or proportion of the total available market or market segment that is being serviced by a company. It can be expressed as a company's sales revenue (from that market) divided by the total sales revenue available in that market. It can also be expressed as a company's unit sales volume (in a market) divided by the total volume of units sold in that market.

a. Marketing plan
b. Business-to-business
c. Market share
d. Green marketing

42. _________ is an inventory strategy that strives to improve the return on investment of a business by reducing in-process inventory and its associated carrying costs. To meet _________ objectives, the process relies on signals between different points in the process. This means the process is often driven by a series of signals, or Kanban , which tell production when to make the next part. Kanban are usually 'tickets' but can be simple visual signals, such as the presence or absence of a part on a shelf. Implemented correctly, _________ can dramatically improve a manufacturing organization's return on investment, quality, and efficiency.

a. 28-hour day
b. 33 Strategies of War
c. 1990 Clean Air Act
d. Just-in-time

43. _________ is a habitual pattern of absence from a duty or obligation.

Frequent absence from the workplace may be indicative of poor morale or of sick building syndrome. However, many employers have implemented absence policies which make no distinction between absences for genuine illness and absence for inappropriate reasons.

a. A Stake in the Outcome
b. A4e
c. Emanation of the state
d. Absenteeism

44. In a human resources context, _________ or labor _________ is the rate at which an employer gains and loses employees. Simple ways to describe it are 'how long employees tend to stay' or 'the rate of traffic through the revolving door.' _________ is measured for individual companies and for their industry as a whole. If an employer is said to have a high _________ relative to its competitors, it means that employees of that company have a shorter average tenure than those of other companies in the same industry.

a. Ten year occupational employment projection
b. Continuous
c. Career portfolios
d. Turnover

45. _________ is a method by which the job performance of an employee is evaluated _________ is a part of career development.

_________s are regular reviews of employee performance within organizations

Generally, the aims of a _________ are to:

- Give feedback on performance to employees.
- Identify employee training needs.
- Document criteria used to allocate organizational rewards.
- Form a basis for personnel decisions: salary increases, promotions, disciplinary actions, etc.
- Provide the opportunity for organizational diagnosis and development.
- Facilitate communication between employee and administraton
- Validate selection techniques and human resource policies to meet federal Equal Employment Opportunity requirements.

A common approach to assessing performance is to use a numerical or scalar rating system whereby managers are asked to score an individual against a number of objectives/attributes. In some companies, employees receive assessments from their manager, peers, subordinates and customers while also performing a self assessment.

a. Personnel management
b. Progressive discipline
c. Human resource management
d. Performance appraisal

46. The term _________ was created by President Lyndon B. Johnson when he signed Executive Order 11246 on September 24, 1965, created to prohibit federal contractors from discriminating against employees on the basis of race, sex, creed, religion, color, or national origin. In more recent times, most employers have also added sexual orientation to the list of non-discrimination.

The Executive Order also required contractors to implement affirmative action plans to increase the participation of minorities and women in the workplace.

a. A4e
b. A Stake in the Outcome
c. AAAI
d. Equal Employment Opportunity

47. _________ is an area of business concerned with the production of goods and services, and involves the responsibility of ensuring that business operations are efficient in terms of using as little resource as needed, and effective in terms of meeting customer requirements. It is concerned with managing the process that converts inputs (in the forms of materials, labour and energy) into outputs (in the form of goods and services.)

Operations traditionally refers to the production of goods and services separately, although the distinction between these two main types of operations is increasingly difficult to make as manufacturers tend to merge product and service offerings.

a. AAAI
b. A4e
c. Operations management
d. A Stake in the Outcome

48. _________ is the use of computer-based software tools that assist engineers and machinists in manufacturing or prototyping product components. Its primary purpose is to create a faster production process and components with more precise dimensions and material consistency, which in some cases, uses only the required amount of raw material (thus minimizing waste), while simultaneously reducing energy consumption. CAM is a programming tool that makes it possible to manufacture physical models using computer-aided design (CAD) programs.

a. 1990 Clean Air Act
b. 33 Strategies of War
c. 28-hour day
d. Computer-aided manufacturing

49. _________ can be defined as the idea generation, concept development, testing and manufacturing or implementation of a physical object or service. _________ers conceptualize and evaluate ideas, making them tangible through products in a more systematic approach. The role of a _________er encompasses many characteristics of the marketing manager, product manager, industrial designer and design engineer.

a. Adam Smith
b. Product design
c. Affiliation
d. Abraham Harold Maslow

50. _________ is an advertisement in which a particular product specifically mentions a competitor by name for the express purpose of showing why the competitor is inferior to the product naming it.

This should not be confused with parody advertisements, where a fictional product is being advertised for the purpose of poking fun at the particular advertisement, nor should it be confused with the use of a coined brand name for the purpose of comparing the product without actually naming an actual competitor. ('Wikipedia tastes better and is less filling than the Encyclopedia Galactica.')

In the 1980s, during what has been referred to as the cola wars, soft-drink manufacturer Pepsi ran a series of advertisements where people, caught on hidden camera, in a blind taste test, chose Pepsi over rival Coca-Cola.

a. 28-hour day
b. 33 Strategies of War
c. 1990 Clean Air Act
d. Comparative advertising

51. A _________ system is a manufacturing system in which there is some amount of flexibility that allows the system to react in the case of changes, whether predicted or unpredicted. This flexibility is generally considered to fall into two categories, which both contain numerous subcategories.

The first category, machine flexibility, covers the system's ability to be changed to produce new product types, and ability to change the order of operations executed on a part. The second category is called routing flexibility, which consists of the ability to use multiple machines to perform the same operation on a part, as well as the system's ability to absorb large-scale changes, such as in volume, capacity, or capability.

a. Jidoka
b. Flexible manufacturing
c. Homeworkers
d. Manufacturing resource planning

52. _________ is the strategic and coherent approach to the management of an organisation's most valued assets - the people working there who individually and collectively contribute to the achievement of the objectives of the business. The terms '_________' and 'human resources' (HR) have largely replaced the term 'personnel management' as a description of the processes involved in managing people in organizations. In simple sense, _________ means employing people, developing their resources, utilizing, maintaining and compensating their services in tune with the job and organizational requirement.

a. Human Resource Management
b. Revolving door syndrome
c. Progressive discipline
d. Job knowledge

53. The _________ Automobile Company is an automobile manufacturer based in Wolfsburg, Germany, and is the original brand within the _________ Group, as well as the largest brand by sales volume.

_________ means 'people's car' in German, in which it is pronounced . Its current tagline or slogan is Das Auto .

a. Competence-based Strategic Management
b. Turnover
c. Volkswagen
d. Rate of return

54. _________ is a term applied to an organization that has created the processes, tools, and training to enable it to respond quickly to customer needs and market changes while still controlling costs and quality.

An enabling factor in becoming an agile manufacturer has been the development of manufacturing support technology that allows the marketers, the designers and the production personnel to share a common database of parts and products, to share data on production capacities and problems -- particularly where small initial problems may have larger downstream effects. It is a general proposition of manufacturing that the cost of correcting quality issues increases as the problem moves downstream, so that it is cheaper to correct quality problems at the earliest possible point in the process.

a. A4e
b. A Stake in the Outcome
c. AAAI
d. Agile manufacturing

55. _________ in engineering is a method of manufacturing in which the entire production process is controlled by computer. The traditional separated process methods are joined through a computer by CIM. This integration allows that the processes exchange information with each other and they are able to initiate actions.

a. 1990 Clean Air Act
b. 28-hour day
c. 33 Strategies of War
d. Computer-integrated manufacturing

56. _________, commonly known as e-commerce, consists of the buying and selling of products or services over electronic systems such as the Internet and other computer networks. The amount of trade conducted electronically has grown extraordinarily with widespread Internet usage. The use of commerce is conducted in this way, spurring and drawing on innovations in electronic funds transfer, supply chain management, Internet marketing, online transaction processing, electronic data interchange (EDI), inventory management systems, and automated data collection systems.

a. Electronic commerce
b. Online shopping
c. A Stake in the Outcome
d. A4e

57. _________ is the process of determining the production capacity needed by an organization to meet changing demands for its products. In the context of _________, 'capacity' is the maximum amount of work that an organization is capable of completing in a given period of time.

A discrepancy between the capacity of an organization and the demands of its customers results in inefficiency, either in under-utilized resources or unfulfilled customers.

a. Remanufacturing
b. Productivity
c. Scientific management
d. Capacity planning

58. _________ is an operational activity which does an aggregate plan for the production process, in advance of 2 to 18 months, to give an idea to management as to what quantity of materials and other resources are to be procured and when, so that the total cost of operations of the organization is kept to the minimum over that period.

The quantity of outsourcing, subcontracting of items, overtime of labor, numbers to be hired and fired in each period and the amount of inventory to be held in stock and to be backlogged for each period are decided. All of these activities are done within the framework of the company ethics, policies, and long term commitment to the society, community and the country of operation.

a. Earned Schedule
b. Earned value management
c. A Stake in the Outcome
d. Aggregate planning

59. _________ or lean production, which is often known simply as 'Lean', is a production practice that considers the expenditure of resources for any goal other than the creation of value for the end customer to be wasteful, and thus a target for elimination. Working from the perspective of the customer who consumes a product or service, 'value' is defined as any action or process that a customer would be willing to pay for. Basically, lean is centered around creating more value with less work.

a. Six Sigma
b. Lean Manufacturing
c. Production line
d. Theory of constraints

60. _________ concern the operation of a facility, as opposed to maintenance, supply and distribution, health, and safety, emergency response, human resources, security, information technology and other infrastructural support organizations.

Personnel that make up 'operations' are

- operators
- engineers
- technicians
- management

This is mainly in a manufacturing setting.

a. Manufacturing operations
b. Labor intensive
c. Market niche
d. Conglomerate merger

61. _________ are goods that have completed the manufacturing process but have not yet been sold or distributed to the end user.

Manufacturing has three classes of inventory:

1. Raw material
2. Work in process
3. _________

A good purchased as a 'raw material' goes into the manufacture of a product. A good only partially completed during the manufacturing process is called 'work in process'. When the good is completed as to manufacturing but not yet sold or distributed to the end-user is called a 'finished good'.

a. 28-hour day
b. 1990 Clean Air Act
c. Reorder point
d. Finished goods

62. The _________ is the level of inventory when a fresh order should be made with suppliers to bring the inventory up by the Economic order quantity ('EOQ'.)

The _________ for replenishment of stock occurs when the level of inventory drops down to zero. In view of instantaneous replenishment of stock the level of inventory jumps to the original level from zero level.

a. Finished goods
b. 28-hour day
c. 1990 Clean Air Act
d. Reorder point

63. _________ is defined by APICS as a method for the effective planning of all resources of a manufacturing company. Ideally, it addresses operational planning in units, financial planning in dollars, and has a simulation capability to answer 'what-if' questions and extension of closed-loop _________. Manufacturing resource planning (or Manufacturing resource planning2) - Around 1980, over-frequent changes in sales forecasts, entailing continual readjustments in production, as well as the unsuitability of the parameters fixed by the system, led _________ (Material Requirement Planning) to evolve into a new concept : _________ (e.g. _________ 2)

This is not exclusively a software function, but a marriage of people skills, dedication to data base accuracy, and computer resources.

a. Jidoka
b. MRP II
c. Homeworkers
d. Manufacturing resource planning

64. A _________ is a type of bar chart that illustrates a project schedule. _________s illustrate the start and finish dates of the terminal elements and summary elements of a project. Terminal elements and summary elements comprise the work breakdown structure of the project.

a. Gantt chart
b. 33 Strategies of War
c. 28-hour day
d. 1990 Clean Air Act

65. The Program (or Project) Evaluation and Review Technique, commonly abbreviated _________, is a model for project management designed to analyze and represent the tasks involved in completing a given project.

_________ is a method to analyze the involved tasks in completing a given project, specially the time needed to complete each task, and identifying the minimum time needed to complete the total project.

_________ was developed primarily to simplify the planning and scheduling of large and complex projects.

a. 33 Strategies of War
b. 1990 Clean Air Act
c. 28-hour day
d. PERT

66. A _________ or transnational corporation is a corporation or enterprise that manages production or delivers services in more than one country. It can also be referred to as an international corporation.

The first modern _________ is generally thought to be the Dutch East India Company, established in 1602.

a. Financial Accounting Standards Board
b. Multinational corporation
c. Command center
d. Small and medium enterprises

67. _________ is the process by which the activities of an organisation, particularly those regarding decision-making, become concentrated within a particular location and/or group.

a. Corner office
b. Chief operating officer
c. Product innovation
d. Centralization

68. _________ is the process of dispersing decision-making governance closer to the people or citizen. It includes the dispersal of administration or governance in sectors or areas like engineering, management science, political science, political economy, sociology and economics. _________ is also possible in the dispersal of population and employment.

a. Decentralization
b. Frenemy
c. Formula for Change
d. Business plan

69. _________ is a type of trade policy that allows traders to act and transact without interference from government. Thus, the policy permits trading partners mutual gains from trade, with goods and services produced according to the theory of comparative advantage.

Under a _________ policy, prices are a reflection of true supply and demand, and are the sole determinant of resource allocation.

a. Free Trade
b. 1990 Clean Air Act
c. 33 Strategies of War
d. 28-hour day

70. _________ is a designated group of countries that have agreed to eliminate tariffs, quotas and preferences on most (if not all) goods and services traded between them. It can be considered the second stage of economic integration. Countries choose this kind of economic integration form if their economical structures are complementary.

a. 33 Strategies of War
b. 28-hour day
c. 1990 Clean Air Act
d. Free trade area

71. The _________ is a trilateral trade bloc in North America created by the governments of the United States, Canada, and Mexico. The agreement creating the trade bloc came into force on January 1, 1994. It superseded the Canada-United States Free Trade Agreement between the U.S. and Canada.

a. Trade union
b. North American Free Trade Agreement
c. Business war game
d. Career portfolios

72. A _________ is a set of exclusive rights granted by a state to an inventor or his assignee for a limited period of time in exchange for a disclosure of an invention.

The procedure for granting _________s, the requirements placed on the _________ee and the extent of the exclusive rights vary widely between countries according to national laws and international agreements. Typically, however, a _________ application must include one or more claims defining the invention which must be new, inventive, and useful or industrially applicable.

a. Food, Drug, and Cosmetic Act
b. Federal Trade Commission Act
c. Labor Management Reporting and Disclosure Act
d. Patent

73. A _________ is a distinctive sign or indicator used by an individual, business organization, or other legal entity to identify that the products and/or services to consumers with which the _________ appears originate from a unique source and to distinguish its products or services from those of other entities.

a. Succession planning
b. Virtual team
c. Kanban
d. Trademark

74. _________ is an idea in the field of Organizational studies and management which describes the psychology, attitudes, experiences, beliefs and Values (personal and cultural values) of an organization. It has been defined as 'the specific collection of values and norms that are shared by people and groups in an organization and that control the way they interact with each other and with stakeholders outside the organization.'

This definition continues to explain organizational values also known as 'beliefs and ideas about what kinds of goals members of an organization should pursue and ideas about the appropriate kinds or standards of behavior organizational members should use to achieve these goals. From organizational values develop organizational norms, guidelines or expectations that prescribe appropriate kinds of behavior by employees in particular situations and control the behavior of organizational members towards one another.'

_________ is not the same as corporate culture.

a. Organizational effectiveness
b. Organizational development
c. Organizational culture
d. Union shop

75. _________ is exchange of capital, goods, and services across international borders or territories. In most countries, it represents a significant share of gross domestic product (GDP.) While _________ has been present throughout much of history , its economic, social, and political importance has been on the rise in recent centuries.

a. A Stake in the Outcome
b. AAAI
c. A4e
d. International Trade

76. _________ is a term used to describe any moral, political that stresses human interdependence and the importance of a collective, rather than the importance of separate individuals. Collectivists focus on community and society, and seek to give priority to group goals over individual goals. The philosophical underpinnings of _________ are for some related to holism or organicism - the view that the whole is greater than the sum of its parts/pieces.

a. Collectivism
b. Collaborative methods
c. 28-hour day
d. 1990 Clean Air Act

Chapter 1

1. a	2. c	3. a	4. d	5. a	6. d	7. d	8. d	9. c	10. c
11. a	12. d	13. c	14. c	15. c	16. a	17. d	18. d	19. c	20. b
21. c	22. d	23. d	24. d	25. b					

Chapter 2

1. c	2. a	3. d	4. d	5. d	6. d	7. a	8. d	9. b	10. c
11. c	12. c	13. a	14. c	15. d	16. d	17. c	18. b	19. c	20. d
21. d	22. a	23. a	24. c	25. c	26. d	27. b	28. d	29. d	30. d
31. d	32. c								

Chapter 3

1. d	2. c	3. c	4. a	5. b	6. a	7. d	8. c	9. d	10. c
11. d	12. c	13. d	14. d	15. d	16. d	17. d	18. d	19. d	20. d

Chapter 4

1. d	2. c	3. c	4. c	5. b	6. c	7. d	8. a	9. b	10. a
11. b	12. b	13. b	14. a	15. d	16. b	17. b	18. b	19. c	20. d
21. d	22. c	23. c	24. a	25. d	26. b	27. d	28. a	29. d	

Chapter 5

1. a	2. a	3. d	4. b	5. d	6. d	7. c	8. c	9. d	10. d
11. b	12. d	13. d	14. b	15. a	16. b	17. d	18. a	19. a	20. b
21. b	22. b	23. d	24. d						

Chapter 6

1. a	2. d	3. a	4. a	5. b	6. a	7. d	8. b	9. a	10. c
11. b	12. d	13. a	14. d	15. d	16. a	17. b	18. d	19. b	20. d
21. a	22. c	23. c	24. c	25. a	26. d	27. a	28. d	29. d	30. c
31. d									

Chapter 7

1. a	2. d	3. d	4. d	5. d	6. d	7. b	8. a	9. d	10. d
11. d	12. a	13. d	14. d	15. d	16. b	17. a	18. c	19. d	20. d
21. d	22. d	23. d	24. d	25. d	26. c				

Chapter 8

1. d	2. c	3. d	4. b	5. a	6. b	7. a	8. b	9. a	10. a
11. d	12. d	13. d	14. d	15. d	16. d	17. d	18. d	19. d	20. b
21. d	22. d	23. a	24. a	25. d					

Chapter 9

1. d	2. d	3. d	4. c	5. d	6. b	7. c	8. b	9. d	10. d
11. d	12. d	13. a	14. d	15. c	16. a	17. d	18. d	19. d	20. d
21. a	22. b	23. a	24. d	25. b	26. d	27. d	28. c	29. d	30. c
31. b	32. d	33. b	34. d	35. a	36. d				

Chapter 10

1. a	2. b	3. d	4. c	5. d	6. d	7. d	8. d	9. b	10. a
11. a	12. d	13. d	14. a	15. d	16. d	17. d	18. d	19. a	20. d
21. d	22. d	23. d	24. d	25. d	26. a	27. a	28. b	29. a	30. c
31. b	32. b	33. d	34. d	35. c	36. d	37. a	38. d	39. d	40. d
41. c	42. a	43. c	44. d	45. d	46. c	47. a	48. d	49. a	50. d
51. d									

Chapter 11

1. a	2. c	3. d	4. c	5. d	6. d	7. d	8. d	9. d	10. b
11. d	12. d	13. d	14. a	15. d	16. a				

Chapter 12

1. d	2. b	3. b	4. d	5. a	6. b	7. b	8. a	9. a	10. d
11. c	12. a	13. d	14. a	15. b	16. a	17. d	18. d	19. a	20. d
21. a	22. d	23. b	24. d	25. a	26. d	27. d	28. d	29. c	30. d

Chapter 13

1. b	2. b	3. d	4. b	5. c	6. c	7. d	8. a	9. d	10. b
11. c	12. d	13. a	14. d	15. d	16. c	17. d	18. c		

Chapter 14

1. d	2. d	3. b	4. d	5. d	6. b	7. c	8. a	9. d	10. b
11. d	12. d	13. c	14. c	15. d	16. b	17. b	18. d	19. d	20. b
21. d	22. d	23. a	24. d						

Chapter 15

1. d	2. d	3. c	4. b	5. a	6. a	7. a	8. d	9. d	10. d
11. c	12. b	13. d	14. d	15. c	16. d	17. a	18. b	19. c	20. d
21. b	22. d	23. d							

Chapter 16

1. d	2. a	3. d	4. b	5. b	6. c	7. b	8. a	9. d	10. b
11. d	12. c	13. d	14. d	15. c	16. b	17. d	18. b	19. d	20. a
21. d	22. c	23. b	24. c	25. c	26. a	27. d	28. b	29. d	30. d
31. b	32. c	33. c	34. b	35. d	36. d	37. d	38. d	39. d	40. c
41. c	42. d	43. d	44. d	45. d	46. d	47. c	48. d	49. b	50. d
51. b	52. a	53. c	54. d	55. d	56. a	57. d	58. d	59. b	60. a
61. d	62. d	63. d	64. a	65. d	66. b	67. d	68. a	69. a	70. d
71. b	72. d	73. d	74. c	75. d	76. a				

www.ingramcontent.com/pod-product-compliance
Lightning Source LLC
Chambersburg PA
CBHW082050230426
43670CB00016B/2845